Susceptible to the Sacred

A sense of ritual has ostensibly vanished from the modern world following the breakdown of institutionalized religion. The importance of rituals as expressions of fundamental psychological conditions was recognized by Jung, but most psychologists have shied away from religious experience in analysis. However, the apparent chaos and pointlessness of life today suggest questions which in turn prompt search and revelation, processes which are themselves a form of ritual. Our religious capacity is thus activated, with or without therapist, companion or priest.

In *Susceptible to the Sacred*, Bani Shorter, a well-known Jungian analyst, examines the psychological experience of ritual in contemporary life through personalized and descriptive images that confirm the place of ritual in the psychology of both the individual and the group.

Basing her book on live material ranging from the consulting room to wider cultural events, Bani Shorter investigates, with great sensitivity, how people perceive the sacred and use ritual in their search for purpose, motivation and transformation.

Bani Shorter is a Jungian analyst in private practice in Edinburgh. She is also the author of *An Image Darkly Forming: Women and Initiation* (Routledge, 1987) and co-author with Andrew Samuels and Fred Plaut of *A Critical Dictionary of Jungian Analysis* (Routledge, 1986).

'We are all susceptible to the sacred. As Bani Shorter so convincingly and movingly illustrates, the sacred is anything but confined to either the Church or the consulting room: it is inherent in life itself.'

Robert Hinshaw, Analytical Psychologist and member of
The Curatorium C.G. Institute, Zürich

'With an approach both broad and deep Bani Shorter argues how the mass mindedness of our modern world has increasingly cut us off from a feeling for our own life's meaning. Weaving a social and political perspective into myths, tribal wisdom and dreams from her own analytic practice she illustrates how this lack of connection between our collective and personal histories often leads to depression, apathy and breakdown. Yet although for many our traditions feel empty and new ways have yet to be found, the author's message is one of hope at the bottom of this Pandora's Box. If we can bear to endure the void of uncertainty, our fundamental capacity to be susceptible to the sacred will be rekindled and we can begin to live in and shape the world from the ground of our own being.'

Elizabeth Meakins, practising Psychotherapist
and freelance writer

Susceptible to the Sacred

The Psychological Experience of Ritual

Bani Shorter

London and New York

First published 1996
by Routledge
11 New Fetter Lane, London EC4P 4EE

Simultaneously published in the USA and Canada
by Routledge
29 West 35th Street, New York, NY 10001

Routledge is an International Thomson Publishing company

Acknowledgement is made to the Ansel Adams
Publishing Rights Trust for permission to
reproduce extracts from *This is the American Earth*
by Nancy Newhall.

Phototypeset by Intype, London
Printed and bound in Great Britain by
Mackays of Chatham PLC, Chatham, Kent

British Library Cataloguing in Publication Data
A catalogue record for this book is available from the British Library

Library of Congress Cataloguing in Publication Data
Shorter, Bani.
    Susceptible to the sacred: the psychological experience of ritual
/ Bani Shorter.
        p. cm.
    Includes bibliographical references and index.
    1. Ritual – Psychological aspects. I. Title.
BL600.S47 1996
291.3′8′019 – dc20   95–3888   CIP

ISBN 0–415–12619–3 (hbk)
ISBN 0–415–12620–7 (pbk)

The book is for Donald, for Tez and for Joachim
each of whom has taught me much,
and it is dedicated
to those in preparation as analysts

Contents

Preface

I am an Analytical Psychologist trained originally in the tradition of Jung. I work with people and their problems. The problems are not always solvable; the people are not always ready to work with solutions. But wherever possible I attempt to link the two, person and problem, in some sort of meaningful relationship.

I remain a Jungian because I have found those basic theoretical perceptions provide an open and honest approach to psyche and personhood, an approach that allows for exploration not only of conditioned behaviour but also of the origins of purpose, motivation and transformation. For ultimately, if one attempts to live with conscious awareness of who one is, these areas too along with unclaimed images of the sacred have to be faced. To me what is termed the self mirrors the unfulfilled potential of being.

This book is addressed to those who find the volatile chaos of today unbearable without asking questions about 'how come?' and 'what for?'. Answers inevitably and naturally involve us with ritual processes of search and revelation experienced concurrently with life development. Sadly, however, most psychologists have shied away from the dimension of religious experience in analysis. For whatever reasons, whether personal or professional, they have not yet found it easy to access and have had no adequate language with which to approach its phenomenology. Therefore, an important aspect of self–world relationships has been largely neglected. It was awareness of this lack, and my realization that as the dream compensates unconscious/conscious relationships, ritual mediates self–world relationships, that prompted my writing.

My interest in how people perceive the sacred and use ritual in their individual lives did not come about solely through contact with those individuals who have sought my help, though it has been fostered and enriched by our work together. I am immensely grateful to the people represented on these pages who have forced me to consider the fundamental role that ritual plays in human psychology. Each of the chapters recalls live experience and contributors have been most generous in sharing fragments of their stories. In so doing, they have offered certain of the most private and most intimate moments of their lives to a mutual search for understanding of the workings of the soul, its resilience and potential. This is a gift for which I and my readers can be thankful.

Because ritual involves the archetype of whatever energies pattern and shape the structure and events of individual lives, its effects are neither possible to predict nor duplicate. We can only try to decode its messages personally and attempt to describe it by way of metaphor and symbol. So, essentially, this is a book based upon personalized and descriptive images that suggest and imply the place of ritual in the psychology of the individual and the group. It is not a how-to-do-it book but an investigation of the ways whereby the sacred core of being becomes activated and manifests itself. What happens when we encounter it and find it speaks in the language of our own persons? – for it is then that we discover ourselves to be susceptible to the sacred.

The book reports incidents that occur in the hinterland between two forces; conformity to outer, conditioned expectations and creative acceptance of the archetypal presence of the sacred. Ritual is the experience of what happens in the space between. Here, with or without therapist, companion or priest, we all find ourselves at one time or another.

Acknowledgements

Various people have urged me to write this book so that its message could be made available to a wider audience than those to whom I lecture, meet at seminars or in my consulting room. I am glad to have had such stimulation and support. I am also grateful to friends, colleagues and others who have been willing to discuss the issues raised here and who have sustained or extended my insights.

But this is not a book based upon either a personal vision or research alone. It is based upon sequences occurring in the lives of actual people, most of whom are alive today. It is they who have contributed the most and to them I am most deeply indebted. In all circumstances where it has been possible to reach contributors, they have been consulted and have graciously given their consent. Descriptions and sequences are accurate psychologically but no-one's story is identifiable exactly as it has been reported. What is true of all portraits is also true here; likenesses are equivalencies.

Conceptually, several of the chapters had their beginnings in seminars or lectures presented to practising psychotherapists or for those training to be analysts. Such presentations were made to students of the Independent Group of Analytical Psychologists in London, to students of the Danish Society for Analytical Psychology, Copenhagen, and to certain others from the C.G. Jung Institute, Zürich, as well as at the Institute of Human Relations, Glasgow. Chapter 6 was first given as the Inaugural Lecture for the Friends of C.G. Jung in Aarhus, Denmark. Chapter 7 was originally part of a Summer Conference programme offered by the Guild of Pastoral Psychology, London. I have felt it a privilege to respond to each of these opportunities.

It has not always been easy to focus upon writing a book of this kind in the midst of demanding circumstances, professional or personal. I would like to extend special thanks to those helpers who have assisted me from the outset. Without them, it would not have been possible. They include Nancy Ault and Audrey Grant as research assistants, my secretary, Marion Ewing, who has worked at the manuscript with sustained patience, as generously willing as she is accurate, and, most importantly, Alyson Carter who has made space and time for me to write at home. I offer my gratitude to each of them, along with a copy reader who first read the manuscript without previous introduction to its content and has worked upon it with sustained dedication and care.

Bani Shorter

Chapter 1

Made by media

Tell me what you create and I shall tell you who you are.
Eckermann, *Conversations with Goethe*

André and Helena sought analysis because they wanted out. There were times when each had felt convinced that he or she wanted out of life itself. Both were employed in media jobs. Caged within studios and offices, constrained by self-referring worlds and confronted by unvarying demands, they longed to end it all. Yet neither could imagine an end other than the one that seemed inevitable. That was death itself. Unaware that what they sought was death to life as it was being lived, each had made a suicide attempt.

Suicide is not a pretty act. In it the continuity of a lifetime is broken, a personalized image shattered. However, the personalized image is but a visible expression of a multitude of invisible bonds that link a person to himself or herself and with a god, however that presence is perceived; for the totality of someone expresses both the given and the potential, individuality and personhood. It is psyche or soul that unites the two. Suicide severs this relationship and denies the furtherance of a conscious soulmaking process.

So there was a connection, I was sure, between the psychological death that accompanies encapsulated selfhood and the suicidal despair of these two people. Though comfortably provided for, they described their days with as little animation as they might have shown had they worked on assembly lines or in sweatshops. How had they been programmed to find such glamorous assignments self-defeating, I asked myself.

The two never met, so far as I know, but nevertheless they

were connected, psychologically speaking. A fantasy of death was their shared reality. Helena despaired of being allowed to express what she felt herself to be as a woman, someone able to rouse, inspire and animate response that would invite a partner to relationship and life. At the same time, without access to such a partnership, suicide was the only 'life' André could envisage.

Helena was recognized as a so-called 'creative' person. Editors or producers were willing to pay a high price for her inspirations. Initially she found the prospect of media work fascinating but gradually she watched her artistry distorted and curtailed by the dictates of the time and space allocated, limited to use of itemized and acquired resources, subject to orders for predefined sequences. Realizing her worth was measured primarily in specific and economic terms she felt increasingly devalued and embittered. 'Imaginatively I was raped and then abandoned,' she said.

Nor had she found that she could anticipate much in the way of feedback from processes once they had been set in motion. She had virtually no contact with readers, listeners or viewers except by way of assessments, critiques, opinion polls and recommendations for advancement or otherwise. Deprived of contact with her public and personal appreciation of the gifts she felt were naturally hers, she languished as a woman/person before her body died. By the time she consulted an analyst, her life was strewn with broken partnerships. She and media man were out of sync. Her sense of personal esteem and authenticity had virtually disappeared. They had been devoured, as if by a computer, part of a programme that couldn't be retrieved.

André, himself a seasoned media man, could be said to have symbolized the force that raped, devoured and abandoned Helena's creativity, albeit without awareness and at a distance. The tragedy was that, in destroying her, he also destroyed the possibility of a vital connection with his own imaginative capacity as well. For awareness of suffering is essential as a prelude to increased awareness and expression of personhood. It is psyche or soul that translates the pain of events into a suffering that impels reconsideration of what more of the larger self requires to be given a place in life. In the case of a man, it does so by way of hints implicit in fantasies evoked and inspired by images of the feminine.

To escape the suffering implicit in soul-change, André had prevented pain entering his consciousness by taking charge of his own images. But fantasy is a natural and essential aspect of being in the world and a way of returning soul to the world through promptings towards self-involvement. It is the manufacture of fantasy that destroys soul and, ultimately, creativity itself. Both André and Helena were employed in the invention and production of imagery rather than the discovery and realization of the meaningful fantasy so essential to psychological and personal well-being.

I second the philosopher's proposition that there is a need to restore to the word 'invention' the double connotation originally conveyed by the Latin *inventio* which meant both discovery and creation. Kearney writes: 'The meanings of our past emerge from a reciprocal act in which interpreter and what is interpreted each contribute to the identification of a pattern.'[1] Without discovery of an underlying process and pattern there is little impetus for change in an individual, yet there is hardly scope for discovery in media invention when the function of reflective insight is foregone and resources are fully concentrated upon completion of a programmed product.

A much neglected area in psychotherapy and analysis is the role played by social history, culture and the work ethic upon individuals. Indeed, it is difficult to identify the point when social history transforms itself into case history and such an analysis is beyond the scope of this book. But analysis can be used as a cultural or historical tool and so doing may throw light on analysis itself.[2] As a method of observation it is a valid instrument of historical enquiry but up to now analysts have been too preoccupied with the empirical validity of their observations to give much credence to their sample. Most of us have neither been prepared to make social commentaries nor have we dared to do so. Consequently, when we have tried to speak about the social context, we have been given to making far-fetched analogies or been prone to over-generalize upon too narrow a theoretical basis.

The present work does not aim at an analysis of current cultural phenomena either. Instead, I simply wish to draw attention to factors which encourage, though not necessarily determine, concomitant psychological responses in individuals exposed to certain present-day social situations. So doing, my goal is neither to evaluate nor blame but further understanding.

Likewise, and perhaps especially in relation to religion, what will become apparent is the similarity of certain approaches which suggest themselves spontaneously within the course of an analysis to other rites and practices, ancient and modern. As I have witnessed and noted such instances over time, whether in connection with my own clinical work or that of those whom I have supervised, I have seen that in many instances such happenings were not prompted by anything immediately traceable in the consciousness of either analyst or analysand. If not due to repressed childhood or encultured influences they inhered in the unconscious propensity of neurotic sufferers to match selected or pathological promptings with clues fed to them by the desire to belong to the inner world of someone else (i.e., they were transference phenomena) or they seemed to erupt from that stratum of psychological life identified by C.G. Jung as the collective unconscious.

When the latter is the case, however, it is no less surprising to the analyst than it is to the analysand and it hardly seems adequate merely to label such occurrences as evidence of an unconscious religious attitude on the part of the analysand. For the manifestation expresses an organismic wholeness native to an individual in whom psyche and religion are co-related and mutually accessible to one another. To eliminate the distinction does not adulterate either one or the other but has far-reaching moral consequences.

Moreover, so far as observances reminiscent of collective rites are concerned, I have found them to be no less valid for being self-initiated. Nor were they always successful any more than what emerged in the course of my work with André could be called successful or proven as a technique, though it brought us to the threshold of awareness of an image that possessed him so wantonly as to be said to have taken over direction of his life. How society encouraged it is another matter.

The psychologist notes that the first symptom of a condition aptly identified as 'loss of soul' in earlier societies is loss of the capacity to fantasize. The cannibalization of information that characterizes today's coverage is equally a cannibalization of imagination and creative potential. The muse is not often referred to nowadays but Bachelard reflects: 'The muse is a notion which should help *to give body to* inspiration and which should make us believe that there is a transcendent subject for the verb "inspire".'[3] The remote and metaphorical feminine is not the all-powerful transcendent subject she has sometimes been interpreted to be, though her image leads to engagement with supra-ordinate potential. Without her, created forms are both artless and temporary.

The enhancement or nourishment of soul that begets inspired creativity is a mysterious process in which the intrinsic wholeness of the human personality is enlivened by a significance which outlasts the production itself. Experience of mythic forms and images touches and combines with personal awareness so deeply and is often darkly felt that it is not immediately accessible to consciousness. By contrast, consciously contrived and pre-packaged imagery is soporific, often devoid of immediate psychic relevance and seldom carries the kind of resonance that is inherent in an encounter with awareness of a 'transcendent subject'. Bypassing the feminine, a purely masculine *inventio* is substituted and it becomes a one-off, making a lasting impress perhaps but not inspiring.

With André, I was involved both with the product and the agency that produced the product. The work of an analyst is to stand with the analysand as he or she is, intuitively and feelingly as well as knowledgeably, being alert to and attendant upon the noetic guidance of what yet remains unconscious to the person. As a woman and from what I have suggested thus far, I remind myself and others that this necessitates giving priority to process and the unfolding of an unexpected, surprising sequence that proceeds inferentially, not from reality to the picture but from the picture to reality.

My brief is to participate in a symbolic undertaking, eschewing the doctrine of an assigned or projected role. Obedience to the feminine content present in the relationship asks that primarily I remain faithful to the metaphorical. This can be assured in no other way than by facing involvement alongside the other while at the same time bringing to my with-standing a similar kind of reflective consciousness to that which is ultimately required (in this case) of him.

Fundamentally, this demands of would-be psychotherapists, of either sex, respect and patience for an imagery forming, neither yet revealed nor rendered instantly obsolete. We remain loyal, that is, to a process of continuing psychic formation and transformation whereby image becomes likeness and in which the symbol is the carrier both of change and meaning. This necessitates, of course, being witness to break-up, breakdown, initiation and transformation as well as at times, unfortunately, suicide. It is not a comfortable position, especially when, as here, we observe a personal pattern reinforced by collective values that threaten the ability of a self-regulatory system to sustain and regenerate itself.

Dependence upon the made image is a threat to the individuality of humankind, whether the image-makers present themselves as political propagandists, evangelical reformers, homiletic dogmatists, media producers or simply sales people, male or female. They are all psychological merchants of one kind or another, for in the modern market place a high premium is paid for invention and the product is assessed by its popular appeal. A price tag is attached, based upon turnover and to meet demand an inflated value is given to the so-called creativity and marketable wisdom of producers and performers.

However, when customer satisfaction is paramount, the dark and harmful aspect of the exchange is ignored. We forget that Hermes, the inventive and wily archetypal force later worshipped as Mercury, god of merchants, was initially acknowledged to be one capable of moving between worlds; glimpsed now as messenger of Zeus but at other times recognizable as one destined to accompany the souls of the dead to the underworld. 'Hermes is the spirit of a constellation which recurs in most diverse conditions and which embraces loss as well as gain, mischief as well as kindness.'[4] If there is a one-sidedness of the conscious attitude that emphasizes satisfaction, a stultifying residue of dissatisfaction builds up in the unconscious.

Here creation needs to be distinguished from creativity. 'Creation means making something new and making it out of little or nothing... creation does not proceed (in the sense of develop),' Barzun writes, 'it occurs.'[5] Creativity he sees as the power to energize that occurrence. But, 'Creative,' quips someone else, 'is industry jargon for words and ideas that go into an ad.'[6]

To their one-sided interference in such occurrences, an increasing number of dissatisfied men and women are awakening and want out. Their responses represent a psychic yearning of which they are only partially aware inasmuch as it is registered as a deeply felt reaction to the paucity – some say 'the indecency', a few 'the immorality' – inherent in the concentration of power to selectively influence the transaction of human values. Still others, interpreting their dissatisfaction from a social and political

perspective, resent the inequality of control that such a concentration of decision-making represents. To the psychologist, however, evidences of unease accompanied by feelings of emptiness
challenge and threaten to overthrow the stability and integrity of
the personal ego, as was dramatically evident for both André and
Helena.

At such a time fantasies of break-up are induced. The majority
of dissatisfied media persons I have met are not yet fully roused
to the psychological implications of their work life. Nevertheless,
they are asking for the iconoclastic experience of analysis in
anticipation of an exchange of assigned and inflated images for
the palpable immediacy of felt relatedness to issues of significance
in their individual lives. Their repressed fantasies are backed by
explosive energies which, when released, might lead to an
increase of individual worth and personhood rather than to life
denial and destruction.

The place that media now assumes in our lives resembles that
of a patriarchal elder, judgemental and godlike. It provides us with
information and ideas and at the same time it counsels us with a
wisdom to which we are expected to conform. In an increasingly
complex world we rely not upon people but networks to interpret
our traditions. That is to say, they directly mediate both our myth
and its meaning. Yet we know that myths of meaning are not
instantly replaceable; they are only renewed by confrontation
with ambiguity, nourished and confounded by the challenge of
dis-ease. A monomyth of instant availability and emotional gratification has its counterpart in a prolonged infantile state wherein
we expect demands to be immediately and gratuitously satisfied.

The speed of media input also discourages the distance and
reflection needed for recovery from the immediate impact of an
experience. For this, time is needed – time to ponder, to assimilate
and to integrate personal implications. Vivid insights act upon
the personality as a spur to restructure our historical sequence
within a framework of newly constellated meaning; they do not
immediately wipe the slate clean, clear the screen or change the
subject. When he himself was interviewed, a seasoned television
interviewer concluded: 'The worst words ever uttered on the box
are, "I'm sorry; this is all we have time for." '[7]

It now becomes relevant to review what finally prompted
André to make his first appointment with an analyst. He did not
choose to do so but had been asked to prepare a series describing

suicide. He had spent 'hours, days, weeks on the blasted project' (his words); trying to get the staging right, finding models, gathering and arranging properties, making sure the lighting was effective, scheduling takes, developing and selecting prints. 'God, I've spent a small fortune on this one project,' he admitted angrily, 'only to have it turned down in the end. What's wrong with it?' he asked me. 'They've said it's too graphic. You ought to know,' he insisted as he showed me some of the shots. 'Tell me. What more could they ask for?'

My immediate felt but silent response was, 'an engagement with humanity'. This was a shocking collage but lacked the impress of humane sentiment. As a consequence, my sympathies were inevitably drawn not to the subject of the takes but to the producer and image-maker himself.

Suicide is a tragic event and those who witness it witness an end or collapse of an individual life. It is a haunting statement in which the mystery of someone's being is exposed; the summation of a person's hopes, despairs, beliefs and potential. Every psychological break-up is a plea for renewal. Some intense shock to the feelings necessitates reflection on one's attitude to the world and one's gods, compelling the abandonment of the given and a search for new possibilities. But in these pictures the outer construct was void of inner relevance.

Analysis is often referred to as 'the talking profession' yet, it seems to me, analysis is less concerned with talking than with listening. For those now wakened to dissatisfaction with various aspects of their lives in a media culture, it is this that analysis can most responsibly offer, a form of alternative listening that involves attentive observation, waiting, hearing, discernment and reflection that is less aimed at replacement than with shift, gradation, transition, continuity and coherence. Analysis and analysts listen, that is, to the subtle shifts of feeling and perception that inhere in the processes of the psychic movement in an individual's life. Therefore, they listen inevitably and naturally to someone's own unique language, however that is expressed. They listen both to person and to psyche. As an analyst I accept that 'to hear faithfully is my concern; I have no other'.

Analysis could provide André much needed privacy, I realized, an intimate space in which he might begin to discover inwardness. In silence perhaps he could enter a realm no longer auto-observant. For though the subconscious is ceaselessly murmuring, like a spring, the source of his dissatisfaction and disassociation was out of hearing, out of sight, beyond his reach. So at first I was conscious of listening as if for both of us, not unaware of the analogous mother/infant relationship in the containment of which the soul or psyche preoccupies itself in preparation for life. It is the time when the contents that explain are less relevant than the images forming which, in turn, inform the growth of individual consciousness.

I had no desire to reinforce the isolation of this man's alienated state but neither should my presence reinforce dependencies akin to subjugation. It is the subtlety of a spontaneous intervention, act or reverie that revives the source and opens a guarded image to regeneration. One must restrain oneself, I feel, from giving commands to personal fantasy.

At a time of dark despair, however, at the soul's midnight, as it were, when confidence is at its lowest ebb there is neither hope nor inspiration, plan nor apparent purpose. Nothing then appears to be more relevant, certainly nothing more demanding than the insistent inner voice that haunts one and asks to be given a hearing. But that is also the time when a chastising mother will blame; a nourishing one will try to succour; a woman driven by habituated animus impulses will judge; a seductress entice. Would I be allowed to speak with my own voice and avoid being cast in an archetypal role?

I remembered another analysand. 'I am ageing,' he had said. 'I am becoming an old man. It's too late.' Such words can be reported as fact and, once reported, with journalistic impact they touch a common chord of human sympathy. The fantasy of the reader conjures an identity with this condition. But, for the analyst, a case is not simply a report. It is *someone*. The analysand tells a living story that reveals a clinical confrontation with a pathology that is universal but here newly and uniquely manifest. His words suggested more than a collective and archetypal summary.

This man, Leo, had been exposed to manipulation all his life. His grandmother, a bulwark of respectability, had mediated his childhood. Thus, he had been held a captive audience in the studio of tradition. 'Most precious', her name for him, was an intentional image. His mother did not embrace him; when he was bathed, she wore rubber gloves.

Later, the church took over as producer/director. By it, Leo was further programmed. It asked of him everything but individuality and to it he surrendered, letting flow, as if through a conduit, the coverage demanded of performer, minister, preacher. During the 1960s, feeling rebellious, he had picked up the message of the moment as change; separation, doing his own thing, living loose, letting it happen, finding his own style. But then? – the sorrowful realization that there wasn't much more time and hence the sad pronouncement upon himself ending with, 'So why bother?' He too had wanted 'out' at that time.

By way of amplification of the processes of men's maturation I return to the telling terms in which a pre-modern tribe described the pattern of adolescent initiation. At that time, they said, women were *grown*, as from a seed, but men were *made* as if in fulfilment of a design.[8] The one suggests an unfolding; the other a discernment of purpose. For both boys and girls this involves a natural uprooting, separation from an all-pervasive maternally centred world and increasing consciousness of an internalized imagery re-forming.

Reformation is in this case rediscovery but the discovery involves confronting one's internalized imagery under altered circumstances. To be initiated is to be re-wed to one's own metaphor, who one is and with a notion of for what purpose. The shift comes about by way of a ritual involving the moral patience to search through the impurities of acquired consciousness for words sufficient to govern one's changed being. Hence, young male initiates were described as dying to childhood to be reborn as persons acquainted with their own visions, fantasies of a spirit world and suppositions regarding its meaning. When mothers greeted their sons after the ceremonies, they no longer recognized them as the little boys they had known. They now belonged to the world of men.

What happens in the last decade of the twentieth century? What are the ingredients blended in the process of making men in modern societies, men who come from such different cultures, persons who have been nurtured in drastically altered circumstances? And what is expected of today's women – mothers, sisters, lovers, teachers and therapists at the time when boys are ready to confront their manhood? Unless they consciously seek it and are willing to pay its costs, today's adolescents do not often set forth equipped with receptivity for the imaginative gifts provided by previous ritual containment nor are they allowed time and space for realization of their governing images.

Instead, during their teenage years, they are almost immediately thrust into the environment of a mega-monoculture where change is mediated irrespective of their roots. More often than not they enter manhood without the benefit of a natural maternal environment and equipped primarily with the remnants of acquired patriachal attitudes, attitudes which now show themselves in need of drastic renewal. With little respect for the irrational and metaphorical – myth, symbol, dream and parable, men being made find themselves without consciousness of purpose and ill-prepared for awareness of inner motivations and conflicts.

To an alarming degree men born since the Second World War have been suckled, comforted, informed, inspired by images on a screen expressive of reference points chosen more or less at random and transmitted electronically. For many now in the fullness of years their most telling emotional and intellectual encounters along with whatever interpretations or insights might be derived have taken place in front of television screens. The manufactured and transient image has supplanted personal confrontation.

Thus, they are not strangers to scenes of horror, death, rape, killing, lovemaking, sex, marriage, birth, pageantry and ritual observance but these events have been presented outside an individual context that would foster reflection and tease out disclosures of significance. Only a few have had the benefit of participation in men's groups which are in any way equivalent to a tribal 'man's house'. Most have introjected their fears and questions, to bear them in secret or to act them out. Repressed or projected, these same fears and questions have become soul problems. Anima unborn is metaphor unformed and unrecognizable in their lives.

I should note that this obtains not only for men (though the problem manifests differently with men) but also for women and it obtains equally for those who may have lived in families who have never owned television sets. The prevailing attitudes of our time are engendered by images consciously assembled and transmitted – attitudes to what is desirable, urgent, affordable, necessary, 'in' and significant. Yet we know psychologically that our only way of altering and expanding perception of the real is by encounter with ambiguity and that myth unauthenticated by personal awareness is paralysing and destructive. A dichotomy presently exists between that to which we give common witness and our myth of meaning.

Here, a commentary from Jung appears relevant:

> ... but what we have left behind are only verbal spectres, not the psychic facts that were responsible for the birth of the gods. We are still as much possessed by autonomous psychic contents as if they were Olympians. Today they are called phobias, obsessions, and so forth; in a word, neurotic symptoms. The gods have become diseases; Zeus no longer rules Olympus but rather the solar plexus and produces curious specimens for the doctor's consulting room, or disorders the brains of politicians and journalists who unwittingly let loose psychic epidemics on the world.[9]

To be receptive is to be vulnerable. Nevertheless, women are now struggling to recover and affirm a receptivity to the mystery of archetypal experience analogous to that which enabled tribal mothers to stand apart and with lowered eyes as their sons moved off to claim an interior vision which only later was apparent in word and deed. At that time, when someone withdraws in search of his own being, it is important that woman remains still and silent lest her living voice sound more loudly than what whispers within him.

To stand aside and allow *dis-solutio* in service to ends not yet disclosed, hidden and unconscious, challenges a woman's faith in the initiate's process, her own person and that which she symbolizes for him. It means that her task is simply to remain aware that she will be used as a living symbol, possibly or especially by someone distraught. 'Is it my destiny to offer myself, unknown, to what may not become known?' she asks herself, ' – even when it seems as if a solution I might provide may be lost?'

To abstain, she will have to value the turning more than the road taken, at the same time conscious that the analogy of the experience is a crossroads. Her need for faith suggests the recovery of an attitude essentially religious within herself. In the ceremonies referred to, after leaving their mothers young male novices were held aloft by their fathers and consecrated to the Sky God.[10]

The fully mothered child is equipped with receptivity for inspiration; the sufficiently fathered child is equipped with trust that a new order can be created after loss of an accustomed one. But André was the son of a mother and father who were political refugees and themselves children of refugees. First survival and then assimilation without trace had been their conscious goals. They did not speak about their backgrounds nor did they often mention their past. Their son could not locate their birthplaces on a map; didn't know where to find them. 'Nothing more than curiosity would ever tempt me to go in search of those places,' he said. 'I have no desire to book that trip.' Still, he was now embarked on a psychological journey inevitably and intimately connected with these same locations.

André had been one of three children; there were two younger brothers, one of whom was born when he was twelve. They had all done well but not outstandingly at school. They had played the usual games, bantered and pushed one another around 'quite a lot', been 'reasonably happy, I suppose,' he said. 'I suppose' was a frequent interjection.

Statements about himself were left unconfirmed, as if deprived of a felt connotation for himself, André. He reached no definite conclusions, advanced no causes, had no strong convictions, was unacquainted with conscious choice. He survived with only fragments of a living myth, proceeding by trial and error, following hunches as to what would work, employing suppositions to explain what might have happened or could be assumed to happen in the future. Emotional involvements were few; his interventions were erratic, often sharply critical and unpredictable. He described himself as subject to ups and downs of moods and tempers. Did I ever hear him laugh?

André had made of the imagined an imaginary life and, so, he continued to live at a distance from reality, propelled by assignments. Media work was a symbol of effectiveness for him. He could take the given units and rearrange them. As one of a crew he could go relatively unnoticed and be singled out neither for applause nor blame. His yearnings for the transcendent took the form of sex and drugs. Yet, he was often speechless before women. His ego was in no way an identity formed in response to inner promptings but, rather, a patchwork of archetypal and instinctive urges.

Jung speaks of a man's inner view of the feminine as 'a personification of the unconscious'. Elsewhere he refers to anima as 'the archetype of life itself'. This suggests that the fluctuating moods and tempers which bedevil a man such as André personify the unconscious for him and mirror his relationship to life itself.

These moods, in so far as André was able to describe them, were short-lived, did not invoke reverie, were circumscribed and often directly traceable to complexes; that is, connected with neurotic yearnings which were the result of thwarted passion or attempts to ward off involvement in crisis, to avoid it as if he had no heart for it. Such fantasies as he was able to share were hollow, limited, cut off from a living source. As with the suicide sequence, they appeared to be uprooted from a human connection with anything other than the appearance of things. For example, fantasies evoked when surprised by a beautiful woman did not suggest a sense of something that would have enhanced, enlivened, or resonated beyond the obvious and visible façade.

Like roving camera shots, both moods and fantasies lacked subjectivity traceable to previously involving engagements, particularly those stimulated by childhood experience. Instead of a remembrance of shared mutuality, André's reminiscences of his mother, like those of Leo, conveyed a sense of non-engagement. From his reports I would assume that she had hardly been present. It was true that he was mothered by a refugee but the core image coincident with his acquired anima was less like that of a refugee than a fugitive. As a consequence, life continually escaped him; he found it hard to lay hold upon it. This, combined with the rupture of primary trust in life's nurturing potential kept him always on the move.

A way of receiving and responding to the fragments of his existence as well as the associations involved was one that emerged from the metaphor of André's everyday work. It had its beginnings in a practice to which he was accustomed. He was accustomed to looking at photographic images. He spent hours trying to see into the footage that he produced to discern how it could be cut or highlighted in order to bring out something that would make it more appealing and apparent to a viewer, purchaser or critic. But so engrossed had he become with the end product that he had often been unable to capture the beheld as he so earnestly wished to do.

For that it seemed that contemplation (a word much more often connected with religion than with psychology) was necessary, a ritual discipline whereby one stays with or meditates upon the pattern inherent in the substance until the impress of that same pattern is conveyed to the viewer. In that process, the pattern becomes one with the viewer so that it can be used as an intrinsic guide to the understanding of the nature of the original substance itself. Ultimately, to lay hold upon life, André would have to enter it. But for the awareness of that necessity to penetrate deeper than is possible by the imposition of will alone, I felt life had to be seen and a relationship established to it by way of a shared, deeply felt observation that was absorbing both to him and to another who was mutually engaged with his becoming himself.

Listening (attuning) and seeing (observing) were basic ingredients in this analysis. Both involved word (communication) but talking (sound) was not central. Perception (revelation) was central, however, a perception that was one with the reflection of that which we heard, saw and communicated while the object of our contemplation was psyche itself.

This was new for André. Psyche had been the neglected element throughout the years of family wandering. Its presence was nothing they could account for. Figuratively speaking, it had landed in a suitcase which had been discarded along the way, lost and forgotten.

Mystical writers of the Christian West distinguish among different forms or levels of contemplation but emphasize the effect of the contemplative's encounter with God as one in which the Holy Spirit infuses or becomes one with the subject. It is the conscious attitude of the participant that distinguishes the practice of contemplation from possession or trance in which one's soul or psyche is unreservedly and unconsciously at the disposal of spirit alone.

Psychologically, contemplation can be spoken of as a form of psychic exchange whereby psyche reconstitutes and realigns in so far as it is able in response to a pattern observable as supraordinate yet nevertheless interior to itself. Ascetic discipline alone is insufficient to induce the behaviour changes that result. Nor is there an exchange of archetypal identities for neither image becomes wholly the other. Instead, what appears to happen is a basic shift of the psychic ground of one's being so that surprising propensities become activated and are made available to consciousness. Thereby the totality of a person is transformed by formerly hidden elements now revealed.

In the case of André, the fundamental presence and image of the natural and residual anima became apparent. Clinically we can describe the residual anima as a predisposition to re-relate and revitalize psychic imagery. What too often overlays it is a crust of applied meaning (as is evident in the unconscious conditioning by the acquired animus of a woman, usually the mother) or a sheath of emotion that is unrelated to genuine feeling (evident in conditioning by the unconscious anima of a male or father figure). Words such as crust, sheath or casing suggest something that covers the surface, however, and prevents penetration in depth. If this happens, one is cut off from the roots of one's being.

Developmental psychologists have approached depth by way of the analysis and replay of family conditioning (personal and/or archetypal); theoreticians by way of conceptualization. André himself had previously taken another path which was by way of an attempt to unlock the enigma of life by denying it; namely, through suicide. A different kind of psychological impact is made, a different kind of notion is fostered if the life force is identified as the Great Mother or the Old Patriarch – different, that is, from that to which André's perceptions were attuned. Likewise, diagnostic terms such as 'impoverished ego' or 'unrecognized self' conveyed no emotional resonance to this young man, accurate as they may have been. But the image of the fugitive did, not because it was pursued but when he saw it revealed as himself. 'That's me!' he could say. 'I've been on the run most of my life. The trouble is I don't know from what.' With that picture, suddenly two patterns merged, that of André and: '*I, a stranger and afraid; in a world I never made.*'

A world experienced as remote and hostile to the individual had programmed this man for his media job. An onlooker, depersonalized and unallied, André had been trying to reimagine himself. Suicide fantasies were resorted to as a dramatic way of putting himself in the picture. It was to him at the time the only way he knew of reaching the distant and estranged world from which he had been tracelessly cut off.

To re-establish connection with that world, we retreated to a *temenos* (the *templum* of contemplation), a shared and quiet realm that felt to him like a refuge, a way station, a place where identities were undefined, neither of persons male or female, by colour, nationality or temperament. We approached, that is, 'the void between two thoughts from which the symbols come'[11] and attempted thereby to attain distance from André's compulsion to hide or keep moving. It was essential to do this in order to unite a part of what could have been with a part of what was.

For imagination to produce a unifying symbol, there must first be a *separatio*, a space where psychic attention can shift and focus elsewhere. By establishment of such a *temenos*, we re-enacted the wisdom inherent in the tribal ritual for adolescent boys. The mother from whom André could now withdraw consciously was the one who had persisted in giving demands to his images as a mesmerist gives commands to the somnambulist and tells him to keep moving.

In what Campbell once described as 'the precious moment when two engrams meet' André and I witnessed a blending of thoughts that dreamed and reveries which thought. This did not happen immediately and, in retrospect, one of the most difficult but facilitating elements demanded of the analyst was what I speak of as 'the moral patience' to search out impurities of consciousness. Within the *templum* or *temenos* we had to wait for evidence of an individuality that would signal felt choice. By way of that a man is initiated at the same time he is re-wed to metaphors that give birth to and energize life.

The individual's capacity to make these distinctions is the primary function of an anima image, seeming at times to reflect the self as 'the *spiritus rector* of our fate'. For, as Willeford comments: 'The phenomenology of the self in lived experience is to be found in imaginative products that require imagination to apprehend them.'[12] The acquired or conditioned anima is an overlay but experience of this deeper and innate propensity leads ultimately to personal trust in a process authentically self-revealing, one that can be acknowledged as good for oneself. For fantasies received *in anima* are documents of natural reverie. Through contemplation of this image André received them as gifts of the soul and her reborn image became something like an origin of consciousness for the receiver. In Goethe's words: 'Half drew she him; half sank he in.'[13] Paradoxically, 'out' was then 'in', a message, a vision, an insight which had its beginning elsewhere but could now be freely acknowledged as one with himself.

I pondered long and deeply about why this change should have suggested ritual observance. I was able to translate the case in clinical terms but these never seemed to explain fully what had happened. Was there something hidden in the sequence that was not amenable to psychological explanation alone?

Chapter 2

Instant liturgy?

> The rite of passage is always an awesome experience because it is impossible to predict what its course will be. Although the initiate knows what he is losing, he has no idea what he is taking on.
>
> Girard, *Violence and the Sacred*

'Oh, I see, "instant liturgy",' the young woman remarked as she entered the church hall where a small group were preparing a memorial service for someone they had all known, revered and loved. This person had been precious and unique, not only to them but to others as well. The impact and outreach of his life were unprecedented in the history of the small, traditional community where the visitor had lived as a small child and where these people continued to live and worship. Those content with the prevailing ethos of the place might have referred to the deceased as 'a difficult man' or 'unpredictable', perhaps even 'heretical', but they would have been wrong. He had been deeply committed but to creative change. That had posed the problem.

Now a priest, a poet, the man's wife and a day labourer were rehearsing a somewhat unusual programme. 'Fine!' the newcomer said brightly. 'I'll just nip out and get my violin so I can join in.' Taken by surprise, the others turned to the priest who replied with a gentle smile, 'Oh, no, you won't! You're welcome to join us, of course, but you'd better listen first. There's really no such thing as "instant liturgy", you see.'

So saying, he glanced round at the group. 'I suppose we've been working on this service for a long, long time, maybe years. Rituals have roots.' With this he picked up his flute and signalled for the musicians to retune so that playing could be resumed.

In the moment, the young woman was dumbfounded and felt rebuffed. But the words of the priest stayed with her and later, when she returned to the city, she shared them with me. 'Why did he insist that I should listen first? ... Listen to what?' she asked. 'What did he mean by preparation? After all, I'm a good enough string player. And what was that about roots?' she queried. Altogether the logic as well as the relevance of the incident escaped her. 'I thought rituals came with the church or something like that,' she admitted.

Looking back on that hour, I realize that I have always been particularly drawn to the cast of characters represented in this woman's story. In their ways they suggest the elements of which ritual is naturally composed. They, too, could be called 'roots'. If it were a dream instead of a real, live sequence we would recognize them as *dramatis personae* of the soul. And, since what we encounter is always part of an archetypal story (though the story may not yet be clear to us), we need to explore the sacred face of being as part of us and part of it.[1]

For all of us, the urge to ritualize behaviour is seldom either ordinary or comfortable for ritual conduct seems to be rooted in a deeply felt need to communicate across a gap; it becomes an attempt to translate the language of one's emotional self in terms adequate to the authority of an unknown source. This is the derivation of practices repeated over and over again compulsively while at the same time it underlies those majestic, infrequent and impressive ceremonies that are observed once or at most twice in a lifetime. Someone may or may not be aware of the immediate stimulus of such a basic impulse (certainly the grieving players themselves could not have been fully aware of all that lay beneath their dedication), but the stimulus propels, inspires and guides participation. And, on an occasion when the power of a necessity to express oneself involves approaching another who does not appear to understand everyday language, the depth of the desire to witness and be heard prompts an out-of-the-ordinary effort to interpret.

In Analytical Psychology 'interpretation' is a loaded word. Professionals often eschew its use in so far as it carries the connotation of simultaneous and conscious translation. We do this with foreknowledge that interpretation *per se* is inadequate to convey the relevance and richness of a symbolic message. But here I use the word 'interpret' in the sense that is implied when one speaks of an actor's interpretation of a role or a musician's interpretation of a composition.

Both the actor and the musician make use of emotion as well as intellect, intuition and technique. They are artists and, therefore, as another artist, a painter, writes:

Now life becomes live, sparse and austere, an absolutely polished structure of skeletal simplicity; uninvolved, uncommitted, underworn, deeply and evenly breathed. Its second plot, not life but art, unfolds wings each day to try the air, pushing out perhaps reluctant visions of other lives.[2]

It isn't difficult to imagine that if someone is engaged at that depth and with that intensity communication would readily leap from soul to soul. But ritual messages are also intended for communication with a more distant and incomprehensible vision. What is the genesis of a necessity to interpret a message so fully expressive of oneself to an audience out of sight and beyond sound? This would pertain, no doubt, to the kind of preparatory listening implied by the priest when he indicated to the newcomer, 'We've been working on this service for a long, long time, maybe years.' Time had to be taken before the players could honestly project themselves into their messages.

Perhaps no-one seriously attempts to speak across such a void unless impelled by an impulse that is found to be inexpressible in any other form. Psychologically, our gods are created by a conscious or unconscious fear of aloneness in the midst of unlimited and overwhelming possibilities. Isolated, beyond boundaries, moved by an exigency utterly personal but seemingly inflexible, one senses a solitude almost too terrible to bear. This, of course, happens readily at times of separation and death.

Such primary estrangement can lead one either to God or the devil, to Heaven or hell, but in isolation there is no release for there is no sense of movement. Time stops; so, reluctantly, one nudges forward tentatively although in fear and dread. Expressing oneself is a risk, a risk to which one submits only when there seems no other way. Yet one makes the attempt, having at least a rudimentary faith that one's cry will be heard for otherwise the act would have no reality.

Individually, then, ritual takes root in a sense of aloneness so bewildering and hazardous that one will sacrifice a previous identity in order to make contact with something more and a strength that resides elsewhere. A necessity prompted by these conditions is inevitably attuned to a personal state while, at the same time, a way must be found to direct the cry beyond the circumstances of the moment. We respond to a force within that urges us to break through and 'tell it like it is' and we do so with the tremulous hope that the effort will not be in vain.

Even when taking part in rites that convey neither resonance nor immediate coherence (as was the case with André, at least at the outset) there is a repressed though not inert longing for them to prove effective. For lives affected by power turn to power. What ensues depends on how we define and relate to what we image as power but all transitional rituals are intended, consciously or otherwise, to ensure contact between ourselves, a power residing elsewhere and some kind of renewal.

Here we can sense a difference between programmed and spontaneous enactments. The latter often appear less polished but their message comes across as markedly compelling, honest (even though crude) and sincere. After rituals are repeated, practised and rationalized, regardless of their original intent, they run the risk of becoming stylized and ceremonious. In contrast, rituals like the memorial service that was being rehearsed can reflect an immediate sincerity that communicates a memorable validity.

Not all such observances take place in churches; not all of them are performed by believers. Such observances are seldom structured by conscious design either but evolve through the necessity of facing the parameters of divine/human freedom and that discipline itself encourages humility, an attitude of respect for mystery and obedience. A rite that is mannered and self-consciously staged no longer evidences its genesis as a command performance springing from a human need to communicate with the authority of the unknown and unexpressed.

Remembered, registered ritual participation profoundly alters being and stimulates a rebirth of consciousness. On this both priests and psychologists agree though their theologies may differ. However, they perceive that through and in relation to personal living we strive to make contact with something that is felt to be superior but fundamental to our understanding of ourselves whether we wish to involve with it, ignore it or worship from a distance. That is to say, we do not merely accept life as it is; we make demands of it and *in extremis* we reach towards a power complementary to our human condition that indicates it has meaning. Nor are we satisfied with a single outreach or encounter; we extend ourselves further and constantly in search of deeper and wider meanings to satisfy what we perceive as individual and interior quests.

The sacred significance of things, however, reaches beyond the purely personal and provides a meaningful framework for the whole. In this instance the word we utter initially, whether verbal or otherwise, is a gesture, the implication of which is not yet clear even to ourselves. But behind the word is a supplication and in it is an implied recognition of a superior and divine sovereignty. To this awareness, too, in all probability, 'listening' was directed by the slow-spoken priest. For, rough though the rite may be, that recognition marks it as religious. At the foundation of all ritual is prayer.

Any attempt to communicate with mystery is at one and the same time an attempt to achieve translation of a vertical and a horizontal transfer of significance.[3] Trying to give voice to an estranged condition we struggle with an unpremeditated message that expresses that condition but also transcends the occasion. Hence, within the limitations of our abilities and at a moment of heightened intensity we re-enact the creation of an artist for what we attempt is both reproductive and innovative. Under these circumstances a symbolic relationship is fostered and comes into being. A language emerges that is private to the needs and perceptions of the speaker yet is felt to be capable of response by a remote and unseen partner.

Rite is a form that realizes itself in its functioning and symbol, the inarticulate word, is its medium. Receipt of an obscure reply to earnest supplication may be surprising or disappointing at first but, implausible though it appears to be, the message carries a charge, offers choice, will invite reflection and restores to creation a meaning. It serves as a conductor of an ultimate and archetypal force, representing the participation of the sacred in veritable, actual form. At its core is evidence of a design uniquely matched to the groundplan of our being and invites an encounter which generates sacred history. Psychologically, then, ritual gathers scattered and sporadic elements to transform an undefined sentiment into individual consciousness.

Worship is never absent in ritual observance. It is intrinsic but the worship implied is recognition of energy natural to a patterning force of profound dimension, superior to yet inherent to individual being. All symbolic images of God must remain incomplete yet we suggest and express that presence by way of personhood. Symbolic messages, however conveyed, whether as spoken prayer or night-time dream, serve as a medium for the Word beheld, indicating and inviting reciprocity.

I was given a graphic example of the Word wrongly read in the incident reported by the young violinist. Mistakenly identifying the priest with the transformative energy he represented for her, she was bewildered and angry at what transpired from their encounter. To her, God had spoken in the person of the priest and she hadn't either the power to relate or reject. Because of the blindness of her projection the man no longer remained a symbolic mediator; he became the reality.

Speaking as a psychologist, Jung defined symbols as 'intuitive ideas that cannot yet be formulated in any other or better way'.[4] Symbolic communication acts as a kind of sign language which is resorted to at the borders of comprehension, not selected to please an audience but made use of as the only appropriate instrument available at the time, and it works both ways. For just as a worshipper can only approach the unknowable awakener of being by way of symbolic utterance, the presence of that mysterious other is apprehensible to us only by way of a statement open to many interpretations.

Received symbolically, our most basic and lasting experiences are given a life that transcends the moment and, at the same time, transforms the place of immediate utterance or transcription. In a ritual attempt to bridge two idioms, two cultures, if you like, two principal movements of being come together. Through release of one's personal identity in the hope of communication with the underlying and archetypal energies of transformation what results is not 'instant liturgy' but a metaphysics of the instant. For ritual occurs at the interface of psychology and religion and is itself the conductor of two voices. In the thin space between oneself and what is felt to be one's god, translation occurs. There a unique fit is attempted between an individual's means of presenting himself or herself and the understanding of a divine presence.

If one feels an exchange of messages has been achieved, one's sense of personal meaning, authority and relevance is enhanced. That intuition may or may not be accurate; it may or may not be lasting, but the very fact that messages are communicated symbolically assures that they will resonate. For the power of the symbol does not diminish. If not read as a sign, its suggestive metaphors urge towards infinity and resonate eternally.

The archetypal impulse or propensity to communicate with a god-image is universally observable and the ritual systems to which it has given birth are manifold. So a psychological analysis of ritual must put forward some notion of the needs that prompt communication across such a void. Here the psychologist is able to observe such necessities from one direction only; namely, that of the human person. Yet, whatever our attitude may be towards an image of the originator and protector of our being, we must remind ourselves that ritual language is resorted to because God or our gods and human persons will speak differently about the same thing. It is here in the active attempt to mediate between two understandings rather than in a comparison of choreographic and doctrinal differences between practices that the richness of ritual lies.

Since it is an approach to the meaning of experience as seen *sub specie aeternitatis* we discover that from a human perspective it is a way of pursuing truth, a precarious and unpredictable quest that nevertheless leads ultimately to an inner awakening and change. Since this is impossible to chart objectively, however, no-one can predict its outcome with certainty. It is what becomes available by way of ritual observance that proves it to be lasting, relevant and revelatory in each instance. Until that is apparent we can only speculate as to the source and purpose. Therefore, ritualized actions essentially accompany a search for individual truth revealed in relationship to a mystery indicative of the primary source and author of being, however that presence is described or portrayed.

Symbolic ritual understanding demands work, work in preparation for change, change in ourselves. Psychologically we approach that understanding from one of two perspectives; either in an attempt to discern the logic of how psyche manifests and transforms itself or by way of a search for the causality of the situation. But whichever view we adopt, where is the analyst who does not admit more than once in the course of ongoing work, 'Well, I never would have expected *that* to emerge', or who has not been stumped by the question, 'But why?'. And, indeed, the founder of Analytical Psychology suggested we look to the *telos* rather than the cause and employ what to him was the more relevant question, 'To what end?'

More relevant because it fires curiosity, releases psychic energy and imagination, is capable of fostering hope and implying purpose. The personality is thereby freed from a crippling dependence upon the logical and obvious. Moreover, because the archetypal intention of the 'what for' cannot be ultimately proven, faith is also kindled, faith that there may be an outcome other than one that seems inevitable. Extending his theoretical enquiry, Jung saw the answer to his question as being connected with individuation or fully expressing the person one is capable of being. With these two attributes, faith and a sense of unique potential, the foundation was laid for acknowledgement of the place of the sacred in Analytical Psychology.

From his conclusion Jung implied that persons are by nature religious and that psychology is concerned with how one approaches religion from the perspective of the human condition. How one interprets it from the perspective of an ultimate god is the concern of theologians and priests. That is to say, psychology attempts to comprehend religion as an intelligible and conscious experience though its revelations are first received in the form of often synchronous, numinous and metaphorical communications.

The impress of such communications is, however, apprehended in the ritual experience. When explored in analysis, the outcome is a discovery of being; if received in church or any other place dedicated to the sacred, the outcome is a celebration of being. Sacred and profane elements mingle in each circumstance and the two cannot be split without damage to both. Unless acknowledged psychologically, the birth or rebirth of consciousness is not witnessed as an event and is in danger of lapsing again into unconsciousness. On the other hand, if no celebration takes place, a sequence of sacred unfolding is not consecrated. For, in the final analysis, ritual provides the circumstance for a metamorphosis to occur whereby one substance penetrates and becomes the other in some form.[5]

'Taking in' the sacred is nothing more than seeing it as the pattern fundamental to all other patterns in ourselves, inescapable and essential. It is an acknowledgement that, being human, we are in possession of a godforce as vulnerable, laudable, dangerous, wise as any other of the most basic archetypal forces which we carry within but with a difference – that its strength outweighs all others, interferes with and permeates all other of our stories, is the subplot of all we do. It is not 'the unconscious' but that which calls attention to all that can be made conscious within us.

Since ritual acts as a two-way mirror, exposing the soul of a person to the sacred and revealing the reality of a sacred presence in the human soul (therefore, a penetration along an interface for which we cannot possibly construct a model), no wonder it demands the most fluid of aesthetic expressions, one capable of multiple articulations.[6] And, as we ourselves change, the context from which we attempt to communicate at the borders of the ritual interface also change. The words we will use will not be ones that would have been relevant in another era, either, any more than they would have made sense at a previous stage of our own development. A person's private thesaurus of ritual expression must naturally enlarge and differentiate as circumstances develop lifelong.

Personal cultures, by which I mean the constellation of habits and values that constitute personhood, resist constraint within ritual parameters that no longer correspond to the contours of individual truth or only coincide at certain arbitrary or socially acceptable points. Inevitably, as conditions change, libido withdraws from outworn forms to seek other and more satisfying channels of expression. For many this creates a puzzling and lonely vacuum, however, since, as libido wanes, it seems as though that which was previously imaged as sacred and caring turns a blind eye or moves beyond one's reach as well.

If this happens, the answer is not a formulaic one; i.e., trying harder, swallowing anti-depressants or stepping up the volume by employing more lofty and sonorous phrases – nor, for that matter, substituting commonplace and popular speech. Any of these remedies may seem to be indicated by an outside assessment but from a psychological standpoint, what is needed is the confidence and humility to recognize and respond to a new situation just as it is. What matters to the inner person no longer resonates with the symbolic language in use. Consequently, the apparatus of ritual has broken down.

Ritual is now a word as often overworked as creativity. Its most common meaning today seems to be associated with repetition; it is referred to as 'mindless', suggesting an act slavishly repeated without intervention of thought. 'The nightly ritual of the television' is a phrase one often hears and it conveys a vague sense of compulsion, as if the television set itself demanded to be turned on and we were responsible to the demands of a media god. 'Ritual is dead,' is a frequently voiced opinion.

But is ritual dead? Certainly outward and collective observances have suffered from neglect and by emphasis being placed upon doctrinaire interpretations. Yet the need for ritual and the practice of ritual have not declined. On the contrary, they have intensified and increased as institutionalized forms have lost their appeal and effectiveness.

We have convincing evidence that the longing for and observance of ritual are a human function – deep, natural and ineradicable. When pertinent rites are lacking or foregone, self-devised forms will be substituted to meet an instinctive longing. Not all such performances are appropriate or adequate; some are injurious and harmful. Most are enacted unconsciously. Still, they reflect a depth of yearning and reveal the psychological conditions of the people involved.

Yet one senses a hesitancy about innovation so far as ritual enactment is concerned. Conservative and radical rightly intuit that no-one approaches the Source and remains unchanged. Ritual, after all, involves an exchange of energies and power. During the transfer the resilience and vision of the human ego are tested to the utmost. But whereas traditionalists fear the loss of control symbolized by the overstepping of secure and established boundaries, innovators are energized by the seductive promise of transformation.

Faced with such temptation and urged on by archetypal promptings, it is the degree of consciousness that makes the difference between a wanton display bordering on possession or shows a humility that safeguards respect for the numinous atmosphere of the occasion. Awareness of the psychological prompting behind the urge will not take away the element of risk but may engender awe and a certain restraint when one realizes that the course of a unique and individual approach to the problems of life will be revealed by way of it. And sensitivity, the kind of sensitivity that inspires spontaneous enactment, is an important emotional ingredient in all ritual celebration, exposing what is registered as a lack of harmony between what has been, the prevailing relationship to the sacred that has become established and what it is capable of being. Without sensitivity to that feeling the ritual urge stagnates and humanity is deprived of transformation.

Wherever and whenever communication with a relevant god-image is ignored, censored or forbidden, a compensatory language expresses itself in private, often clandestine observances. The proximity of such rites to witchery and magic correlates with the diminution of consciousness provoked by the prohibition.[7] Aggression and counter-victimization give expression to the pent-up rage of the repressed. But, nevertheless, such rituals are not godless; they are reactions to one-sided, inflexible and inadequate images. If ignorance or avoidance of the divine is fuelled by resentment, an archaic power of archetypal force then erupts. Chaos confronts chaos; cruelty is unleashed against cruelty. How important it is that mediators along the boundaries of the psycho-religious interface bear this in mind, whether they be priests, psychotherapists, parents, professors, politicians, policemen or other would-be helpers.

We find it easy to label, categorize and explain the ritual urge in abstract terms without giving full value to its specificity. For example, depth psychologists will say, 'The need for ritual, of course, proceeds from the unconscious.' But ritual, like creation, does not proceed; psychologically it occurs. Moreover, it is now rather generally accepted that the unconscious is a piece of equipment to which everyone has access. It manifests in primordial and archetypal patterns both recognizable and repeatable though at the same time personally significant and unique.[8] It would be unrealistic to point to any one ritual as illustrative of all that might be said on the subject, as unrealistic as to expect that those who undergo similar observances will be stamped with an identical impress.

The example described at the beginning of this chapter illustrates the dimensions of ritual only in broad outline. It says very little about what the participants believed. It merely reports that they were moved to enact this last rite for their friend in a community where loyalties were divided. Their evident faith was that it needed doing.

Perhaps they presumed that if ritual were respectfully celebrated, something else than what was immediately apparent could break through by way of human sentiment. This might even intervene in such a way as to differentiate and inform collective values. 'Keeping faith' for them was not dictated by habit, though, any more than it signified loyalty to a cause. Instead, it seemed to have more to do with the act of 'keeping faith' with their companion.

To them his life had symbolized values that were endangered in a divided community. We have no notion of what they thought about his afterlife, nor do we know the effect their service may have had upon the community. We only perceive that it sprang from a sense of companionship and grief at the loss of a figure who had exposed himself to the profundity of existence, whose presence had exerted a meaningful influence to which they felt moved to respond with a release of creative freedom for which rite would be the only suitable container.

Merely a description of what occurs in a service is all that can ever be given while to some extent the myth which is contained in the form conceals the ultimate significance or Word though giving it personified expression. Still, the message chosen and sounded by way of ritual endeavour decides the possibility of a myth's being lived onward. In sacred story the Word is ever-present and believed capable of release only in the telling. Unuttered, it loses its power; enacted, it is the thing rendered in a form that becomes a landmark or turning point, releasing it for conscious realization, however its innate symbolism will be interpreted. And, can we ever know the names of the audience, those faceless ones out there to whom the sounds, well or poorly sounded, are a synchronous event, the experience of a surprising moment that will echo and re-echo throughout their lifetimes?

At the core of ritual is an experience of life, death and rebirth symbolically registered that will in turn affect the being of participants in manifold and ongoing ways. The mystery of that intervention defies objectification and analysis. Yet, from the implantations of such moments personhood sprouts and matures in ways that psychologists are unable to foresee or explain. Such interventions are polysemous with the capacity of the same expression to fertilize different meanings.

I feel the term ritual should not be squandered or loosely applied to inconsequential and habituated behaviour. There the better word to use might be ceremony. Authentic ritual enactment concerns itself with transition and transformation; ceremony with the awarding and preservation of status. But, if one applies the term ritual in conjunction with ceremonial performances, credence and value must needs be given to its other aspects as well. Religiously and psychologically use of the term is most apposite for those occasions when mutuality of outreach between personal and so-called sacred worlds is sought and anticipated. Here there is acknowledgement of its being the seedbed of psyche or soul.

Ritual involves the two and seems to be impelled by a desire for a reciprocal connection. To seek ritual is to intentionally interrupt life in hopes of furthering it by making that contact. In the act, the prevailing reason of someone's life is opened not just to question or affirmation but to confrontation, choice and regeneration. It is a submission to creative change and the analogy of love is implied.

The connection of ritual with *eros* is vital. At a time of regenerative change equivalent to a period of ritual demand what is required of an individual is neither correction nor adaption but a leap of faith that is made possible only in response to the dynamic of love since neither impulse nor idea of themselves are capable of love. The ancient Greeks did not speak of love for a god or of a god's love since love itself was assumed to be a god, the oldest among them – Eros, the primal impulse of the universe.

Here we confront a daimon or mystery. The *eros* expressed in ritual is an initiatory love. It is aimed at soul-change and it is a challenging task to delineate between a love which is soul-making and a love distorted by power. Whether the power is seen as being directed towards persons or towards the Source, in either case it distorts and the rite fails of its purpose, becoming a one-sided attempt at manipulation. Again, the efficacy and healing potential of ritual participation are rooted and safeguarded by psychological honesty (not to be confused with consciousness alone) and nowhere is this more difficult to maintain than in relationship to another felt to be the apparent source and reason of one's being.

From earliest times ritual preparation has involved purification, a cleansing of narcissistic or egotistical bias and device. Participation requires discipline and obedience to that ethic, so straightforwardly and simply put by the mediating priest in our story. Collectively speaking, services (in which I might include certain analytic sessions) are containers for personal improvisations involving psychic cleansing and soul-change. To the extent that this is neither admitted nor adhered to, the act becomes decreative and harmful, easily reflective of an attitude that could be labelled 'blasphemous'. Essentially, the undertaking of ritual should itself be a moral act based upon an ethical commitment.

Approaching a partner as remote, hidden and obscure, as firm yet ever-changing as the one envisaged in a seeker's image of the source of transformative possibilities requires the tuning and re-tuning of one's psychological instrument constantly, for the one by whom the composition is ultimately judged is no other than the creator of our being. That such a one is perceived as an archetypal image within one's soul does not diminish that authority; in fact, it enhances it, though I am aware how hard it is for many convinced people to grasp and accept this. While serious psychologists and psychotherapists have themselves abstained from interference with religion, by and large religion has disregarded psychology, accepting it only in so far as it has been found relevant to pastoral care. Fortunately, the imagery of psyche itself makes no such distinctions.

Psyche's image of the Source and Creator of Being is not an intellectual construct. It is a personified companion whose demands must be taken into account and to whose wishes someone is surprisingly prompted to relate. Personification of the god-image is a natural process whereby 'there exists a mode of thought which takes an inside event and puts it outside, at the same time making this content alive, personal and even divine'. Furthermore, Hillman writes, '. . . personifying is a way of being in the world and *experiencing the world as a psychological field*, where persons are given with events, so that events are experiences that touch us, move us, appeal to us (or otherwise)'.[9] It is when our gods are not given place and recognition that they become diseases.[10] Of equal significance, as personified images the gods are given access to our hearts.

'Loving is a way of knowing, and for love to know, it must personify.'[11] This latter is not only a statement expressive of psychological truth; it also has deep theological implications. It says something about the origin of what the violinist was quick to call 'instant liturgy' for ritual is the meeting place of the personified and reality in some form, being the place where realities are exchanged.

In the highly intricate and complex world of today rites are labelled and categorized as primitive, ancient or modern and further identified ethnographically, politically or as belonging to one or another of the recognized religions. This suggests an assumption that growth can be charted in linear terms; it reflects an intellectual and historical bias. Does world history run parallel with society's quest for enlightenment? Doesn't such a proposition indicate an outworn faith in development that was identified with the Age of Enlightenment?

In recent years, it has come as something of a surprise to theologians in particular to be confronted with evidence that persons project rites ahistorically when appropriate to their souls' needs and reject de-creative rites imposed on them from without. Contrary to the assumption that rituals exist primarily to reinforce a collective and traditional order, we find that psychologically they are sought at times of personal transition. From the religious aspect of ritual one derives the insight or revelation which arises from the dialectical interplay of the subjective factors belonging to the individual and the objective fact of the sacred. An individual and spontaneous, as well as a collective and historical, context is germane to their efficacy and survival.

Conditioning sets its own ineffable stamp upon us all while at the same time we sense a hunger to discover and manifest individuality. Yet we find it difficult to unearth the words with which to portray individual freedom – words that are fresh and satisfying. The language traditionally used is never adequate to express innovation; neither does it concur with a deepening sense of a unique subjective role or destiny. So a suitably reflective period has to elapse during which we can withdraw for a while to converse both with our encultured tradition and with the possibility of creative change in anticipation of speaking words we dare call our own. This is a need signalled psychologically by apathy, depression and loss of libido.

The timeless time and private *temenos* of ritual are adapted to meet this need. At that time and in that place one struggles to find a language and employs gestures ripe with many meanings. Ultimately, what satisfies must reconcile both the past and one's yearning for relationship to a destiny contending to become part of the living present. The need for communion and, finally, union with an image of destiny capable of human expression is served only when words are discovered that are felt to be capable of 'carrying knowledge and meaning elsewhere', which was the original sense conveyed by the Greek *meta-phorein*.

That is to say, a metaphor emerges that serves as a uniting symbol between tradition and a future in prospect. We can only hope this happened for the players discovered in the church hall. Its meaning proceeds from a combination of the known and already revealed with the unknown and not yet disclosed. Allowing for reciprocity and relationship between these two, we are then able to explore the dimensions of both symbolisms. If, however, we attempt to master the Word expressed symbolically, and attempt to do so by 'instant gnosis', we no longer wrestle with these dimensions; we reshape and objectify them. If accepted subjectively as well as metaphorically, however, the Word shapes us by revealing new dimensions of imaginable being. A metamorphosis of imagery then occurs which extends beyond the dimensions of the reasoned intellect alone.

So revelation does not come to us only as a surprise, out of the blue or by chance, any more than it is the result of repeating certain cadences, however meticulously. It 'grows' on us and in us, mysteriously conveying a sense of rightness, of grace, a gift received as with a god's intent even though to recognize and make use of the gift imply readiness. Both psychologically and spiritually to be ready is an exercise not alone of choice – that puts it in a bargaining (social) or consenting (political) context, but also of allowing oneself the freedom to know oneself in one's case history and to realize oneself as an individual person.

Ritual expresses the ultimate creative design in the sense that ends are not determined from without but born from union of our existence with a source of ultimate possibility. The same circumstances can lead to other than benign outcomes, certainly, be they addictive, regressive, revolutionary or insane. The difference does not lie in ignorance or deprivation but in an inability to submit the whole person as an equivalence to the frightening possibility of what is acknowledged as possible. In one's inner theatre it is the wholeness of someone who receives and interprets revelation, not simply the abstract, historical, partial or merely the encultured person.

We have now come full circle. Psychologically, to say to the individual that ritual seems to arise from a need to interpret to an unknown Source an inexpressible dilemma, is to say it is rooted in an unfathomable necessity to change. One stands at a crossroads of consciousness and unconsciousness and attempts to express the need for relationship of the two in a language mutually accessible to both.

To 'listen first' will not be to abstain but to recognize that enactment has its beginnings in the challenge faced by being true to one's self-potential. We reach for ritual when our concept of who we are has placed that which would heal or transform us beyond our reach. It is a dangerous moment, a despairing and yet a hopeful moment. What we may become trembles in the balance while whatever there is in life that is bearable, unimagined and contingent is consigned to the enigmatic and meta-real wisdom of transformative rite.

Chapter 3

Theatre of the soul

Holiness is then an art in which gods and men do business with each
other.

Socrates

Our present-day civilization is depleted, exhausted, and nowhere
is this more evident than in our yearning for encounter with the
irrational along with our incomprehension and mishandling of
the rituals that we enact. A self-styled shaman plays to a packed
house in a ramshackle room on the Boardwalk in Atlantic City.
Witches dance in neighbourhood covens. 'Ritual child sexual
abuse' is now a common phrase. Church assemblies divide over
the question of gay and women priests.

It would seem that we no longer possess our rites but are
possessed by them. Not honouring our gods, they dishonour us.
Such chaos is seen as the break-up of what was and it is feared
as a prelude to what may come. Not long ago a child would say,
'When I grow up I'm going to be . . . ,' and say it with a certain
confidence. Now parents are less sure about a future that is in
store for their children. Young people turn to Jung and quote his
final words on the screen: 'The future hangs by a thin thread and
that thread is the psyche of [the human person].' Like Jung, they
equate psyche with soul and they feel the ecology of the soul is
at risk.

Whatever else the foregoing may say about the course of contemporary civilization and culture it suggests that the drama of
the irrational accosts us in many forms. It can assume many
shapes; it is capable of many styles of performance. But its enactments occur at breaking points and crossroads of life; collective
and individual, human and divine, known and unknown, whenever there are attempts to marshal resources for a creative

response to change. So it is not by novelty alone that symbols have the power to attract but it is also by their relatedness to a whole as well; not just to the sacred as if it were split-off but with recognition that it is one with the performance of daily living.

To speak of religion as taking place in the theatre of the soul or psyche is not new but to work knowingly with this awareness present-day religion will need to reconsider its dogmas and psychology to rethink its premises. Neither can any longer avoid consciousness of the other. The assumption by either one that the sacred is tangential has become outmoded. It refuses to acknowledge individual performances as expressive of multiple images and ignores the theandric nature of events that are registered as combining the potential of both divine and human natures.

In today's rapidly synthesizing world people are exposed to and it is now possible for them to explore occult, esoteric, obscure and formerly forbidden religious observances openly and with abandon. This has initiated them into spiritual practices that have direct and immediate emotional appeal. Alienated and estranged from time-honoured services many people have taken refuge in communal forms of worship that are infused with strong ingredients of animism and paganism. Betrayed by scientific materialism they now, covertly or openly, give expression to archaic and tribal practices which were forerunners of consciousness and involve acting out archetypal religious themes. However, these practices too, no less than the routine observances from which today's young people flee, are objectivized, being older than any church. The question becomes how we can consolidate exposure to such rites within a psychological and religious framework that is therapeutically relevant, honest and theoretically tenable.

Stone circles, temples, theatres, cathedrals and all settings invested with experience of the numinous and sacred are hermetic places of exchange where the given changes form and being is born. Here ultimate images play in the guise of gods. These figures are noetic, suggestive, dreamlike, existing as they do in two worlds at once, the psychological and the metaphysical. Along with dreams they become 'transparencies of transcendence' and their symbolism is comprehended as analogous to the human condition. The function of such images is a transformative one. In fulfilment of that function they reveal the person who is and expose the core of the person to come.

It is within the soul, then, that one is brought face to face with the reality of the active, mysterious power of the sacred and the stage for encounter is set within psyche itself. What happens there inevitably becomes ritualistic, transforming the place into a container for personal confrontation with the transcendent and irrational. Feelings will then be aroused with an intensity directly related to the transformation required of the deep emotional self as one's renewed experience of the numinous translates itself into a revitalized and suggestive imagery. The image and concept of God are no exception to this process either for it is itself a metaphor of the unknowing mind yet a psychologically affective and effective image. Religious and psychological life partake in the discovery of relatedness between the two.

To describe what occurs during the transformative time of ritual encounter religions have advanced multiple myths of meaning but as yet psychology has found few authentic words. No doubt, however, the actual experience of confrontation was there for C.G. Jung. He saw visions and he gave them the most adequate expression that he could. He observed; he reflected; he recorded and reports of what he witnessed were incorporated into theory.

He dreamed vivid, terrifying dreams of his encounters as well, dreams that he found so enigmatic that he had to reach for brush or chisel or pen to express, realize, or otherwise to acknowledge, to some extent to control them and thereby lay hold on their elusive and bewildering power. Now, taken out of context, these same dreams lose some of their numinosity and at times it is difficult to grasp their personal impact. But he, of course, did not meet symbols as definitions. They were presences and he related to them, to use his own words, 'just so'.

Archetypes became recognized as live and personified images present in his own unconscious psyche. He found the script of his life presented to him in the theatre of his soul and he read his lines from his dreams. Hence, belief became other than supposition and being transformed into knowledge gave meaning to wholeness. This was also true of his image of the sacred which he referred to as 'the self'.

Some years ago an anguished young woman for whom the future looked very bleak indeed shared with me a dream which now seems relevant. She reported:

'Last night I was in a small theatre. I stood at the entrance to the auditorium, by a door located about half way back. In the front row I could see my mother, my father, my brother and my husband [all of whom had once seemed reliable and supportive figures but from each of whom she had recently become separated and was now cut off]. Before them was an empty stage. They sat there expectantly, waiting for the show to begin. But I knew it wasn't going to happen there. I tried as hard as I could to get their attention. I tried as hard as I could but they just wouldn't turn or listen to me. I wanted to tell them that the play wouldn't be on stage. The real show was a mime show and it was taking place in the shadows at the back.'

I find this a very poignant dream and in its way illustrative of the dilemma of today's youth. I am quite convinced that dreams have collective as well as personal significance, as convinced as I am that the deepest reading of any dream, the most difficult and treacherous but also the most rewarding, reaches to the point of subjectivity where the 'sharp feathered word' of revelation is uttered, a revelation that speaks of the entirety and eternity of one's person/self quite naturally and without pomposity, ignoring delineations between essence and existence or body and spirit. To reach that point we do not have to struggle intellectually but simply allow for the possibility that the divine can become human while we often appear to be inhuman.

Psychologists are often eager, as I was initially, to formulate an explanation rather than to ask in such an instance as presented itself to the young woman, '... and what was the play about?' The answer to that question must be found for each and by each individual and if we were to take it seriously our work, whether as religionists or psychologists, would become less a matter of instruction than an attempt to eliminate resistance to the psycho-sacred process. 'Our way, then, would be a *via negativa* – not a collection of skills but an eradication of blocks', – these words being not those of a religionist or psychologist but a dramatic artist.[1]

I could go on to use the dramatic process as illustrative of the developmental work of analysis or, likewise, I could attempt to analyse spiritual confrontation as ritual drama. Such attempts have been made again and again. But I shall not do that; here my purpose is a different one. I wish to uncover if I can the inherent connection between two hitherto separate approaches, religion and psychology, and I shall do so by an exploration of dream as ritual drama.

I do not want to explore relevance to outer perception but to get closer to the 'how' of its happening, the manner, if you like, by which transformation is effected, a psychological transform-ation that is both lasting and preparatory for further change. In the search for what is not, we begin with a notion that something is missing. There is, I would judge from having practised in cosmo-politan as well as more traditional areas, general agreement that the psycho-religious drama is not on the open stage. It is a mime show taking place in the shadows at the back and, I repeat, I must put to myself the question, 'What is it about?'

Mime shows are inarticulate. Their silence is rich with intuitions of knowing but it is left to the observer to give voice to the unspoken words. Hence, they make demands on us as members of their audience while at the same time we find them evocative and beguiling. Like archetypes their wordless images need human persons to respond, make evident and manifest the messages they carry. Gaps in communication ask to be filled by our individual perceptions and imagination.

Similarly, in a struggle with our own truth it is a challenge to discover there will be times when we are at a loss for words. At a moment of psychic shock we seldom behave predictably. Then a sign, not a conscious gesture, will indicate our condition and the sign can be read as a signal of ourselves.[2] We are reaching for a language we do not know we possess to express a word we do not know we are yet capable of expressing.

Watching a mime show we instinctively empathize with the plight of the performer and find it easier to identify with the signs given by a mute player than with the speeches of an articulate actor. How precise, then, was the image of the mime for someone who described herself as 'speechless in face of the future'. Its show was her show. It was unnecessary to introduce her to the concept of the shadow; she was one with its enactment.

Happenings that occur in the theatre of the soul – dreams, nightmares, fantasies, reveries, visions, insights and revelations, all part of the process of becoming conscious, are certainly upsetting and surprising but by way of them psyche rehearses us for scenes of confrontation, enlightenment and choice. Speaking psychologi-cally but continuing the analogy, it offers a play space in which ego and self can act as co-directors. Authorship, however, essentially remains a mystery. The final production will be an improvisation on a theme, suggested by an unseen partner.

Nevertheless, at the very least, the presence of mystery assures that in some measure the production will be realized. A mysterious and unclaimed power inspires awe, respect, perhaps even dread, any of which may serve to shatter the façade of everyday and commonplace behaviour. The ordinary words we would have used before no longer apply and we are forced to search for a word which signals a changed condition. Taken by surprise we are able to see that our habituated assumptions not only inhibit transcendent living but also lead to it.

Each life première asks for an act of transgression on our part. By way of that transgression a new balance is struck within the personality and a new communion made possible, a live relationship to the god-ness of one's being. This sense of sacrament and community will over-ride the temptation to hybris in light of achievement or the complacency derived from having made a correct or honourable choice. We now leave collective standards behind and a different sense of well-being or fulfilment brings with it a satisfaction derived from being simply oneself and as miracle. We are not the miracle but miracle is within us. We co-exist with it in mutuality. Within the confines of our case histories we catch glimpses of meta-history shining through.

These glimpses introduce us to the multiple patterns through which the sacred can be expressed. They can never be explained solely by the circumstances of the moment but also carry the impress of eternity. From a psychological perspective the experience that is lasting is an experience whose significance is related to a whole. Likewise, though one's point of view is an individual one it partakes of cosmic insight as well. In this regard Jung chose to draw a distinction between the personal and archetypal and he was convinced that a relationship forged between the two was connected with awareness of meaning. Hence, he equated moments of conscious insight with the derivation of meaning.

Here an understanding of the archetype of the self can be easily misunderstood if the self is perceived solely by way of its function rather than as an iconic, constantly transforming and revealing image. Is it the instigator of the production or that which relates an act to meaning by transcendence of the division between subject and object? Our psychological history exists for us solely by virtue of a story which is in the first instance about our own meaning but ultimately is realized to be linked with the realization of the sacred itself.[3]

The place of exchange where meaning is acknowledged is, again, the temple of the soul. This is where dreams begin. It was in the depths of their souls that the prophets heard the voice of their God and it was by way of a dream that the Wise Men were forewarned of Herod's malign intent. But the inspiration of a dream is not yet the show. The dreamer will have to live herself into its message. 'We know', Grotowski insists, 'that the text *per se* is not theatre, but that it becomes theatre by the actor's use of it.'[4] This is to say the dream is neither good nor bad, positive or negative; it is how we respond to it that matters.

In the soul's theatre each of us seems to find ourselves cast successively as creation, model and creator. Psyche becomes the scene of a magnificent drama whose purpose is disclosed by the revelation of the actors when they acknowledge the word that is in them as belonging to the *logos* of their god and not merely a script assigned for the playing of an ordinary or average part. It is received as from the place to which ritual invocations are projected: the reply takes possession of the human condition for its transformation and redemption. Basically, this is what the play is about but, like the mime show, its interpretations are infinitely varied.

How astonishing it is to find oneself cast in a role so bizarre and far-fetched as to be hardly comprehensible. Are we ever sufficiently prepared for that? As with so much else that happens along the way towards becoming an individual, we assume we can grasp the structure of the plot but we hardly surmise the specific sequence. Here we underestimate the ingenuity of an author/ partner of whose design we remain unconscious until it becomes manifest and we are finally awakened to its personal implications.

'In a theatre located in a city where I once lived and felt most fulfilled,' a dream unfolds, 'an old school friend and myself have been recruited as clowns. Our act is to fill a twelve-minute slot in a longer pantomime. We haven't the remotest idea what we will do. The producers keep promising rehearsals which never take place. There are no props but we have been promised balloons.

The time for the performance comes and we are still totally

unprepared. We wait in the vestibule and there we are offered a large square white pill which is supposed to lessen our stage fright. I refuse at first and am then persuaded to take a bite. But when I learn that even the balloons haven't been provided I rebel and refuse to proceed.

The man in charge of the performance is summoned. He is an unpleasant character and very threatening. He reminds me that I have *signed a contract*. The door into the wings opens. I can glimpse the stage and the audience beyond. I know it is time to go on.'

This is living theatre and bears a strong resemblance to the work of a theatre group that for a while most exemplified the search for meaning prevalent in the 1970s. Calling themselves The Living Theatre, its interpreters struggled to free actors' inhibitions and prejudices by erasing the barrier between audience and players, thus hoping to create a humanizing atmosphere.

We have to shake off the sophistication of our time by which we close ourselves up and become vulnerable again.... We've closed off a great deal of our total human response but as actors we must open up again, become naive, innocent, and cultivate our deeper climates – our dread, for example. Only then will we be able to find new ways to express the attitudes which we hold in common with the outside world and ways to express the attitudes which we hold uniquely.[5]

In his statement Joseph Chaikin might have been anticipating certain of the implications of the reported dream. For the clown represents the opposite of well-ordered ego performance. With haunting naïvety he exposes the fragility of the human condition. He blunders; he is not the master of a situation; he is vulnerable; he is innocent; he evokes pity. 'Who is the clown?' ask Ann and Barry Ulanov. 'He who tells us that only by way of this human life do we know the mystery of being. Only by accepting our human-ness can we open ourselves to God.'[6]

This puts a different look upon the dream and, indeed, upon the act of dreaming. Do all dreams open ways to God or does this happen only with receipt of an outrageous and seemingly out of character summons? Is it a punishment or a reward, then, to be cast in the part of the fool? Probably neither. Whether or how the part is accepted will depend upon the dreamer's own response and the clown, after all, is an archetypal image replete with possibilities for a variety of interpretations, both positive and negative. But for an untutored actor to attempt to play it at all will necessitate a sequence of transformation involving two uniquely powerful and private images at one and the same time; the first, a previously held image of personal identity and the other an image of the author of one's being.

Whether or not the assignment is completed, whether or not it is undertaken willingly or otherwise, as the dream dreams itself onward a ritual unfolding of life, death and rebirth must proceed, reflective in some way of a symbolic death and rebirth of one's saviour–god. The dream cannot now be undreamed and its plot requires the dreamer to acknowledge the psychic possibility of involvement with that so human and in so many ways terrifying part on a familiar stage but without props or previous preparation. No props, only the promise of balloons; nothing tangible or actual, only symbols of fantasy, ideals and hopes.

To play the clown will be to divest oneself of the familiar trappings of everyday life; status, persona, recognition and position. Likewise, the portrayal includes divesting oneself of personal feelings attached to these attributes as well. One sheds them like ill-fitting garments or masks to become a medium for the emotions that beset us all, a container and communicator of the censored and chaotic feelings that well up and betray us, hanging loose and spilling over when we stumble upon the enigma and imbalance of life. By the repetition of useless and fruitless gestures the clown personifies and ritualizes the limitations of our solely human response to the confusion and wonder of change, challenge and initiation. He or she reveals the primordial human reaction when face to face with the unthinkable god-thought.

Again I am struck by the precision of the dream. The act will be played for a brief but specified time which interposes a break in another and ongoing production. Exactly twelve minutes are allotted, twelve minutes for someone to wear white-faced anonymity, undeclared, adrift, to suffer the relief and trepidation when divested of previous faces and poses, other costumes and expectations or, faithful to the ambiguity of the text, to stagger across the stage of liminality without props, bereft of identity, not having found a connection to a renewed self, a vagrant and an outsider, a fringe character, a border person, recipient of multiple projections. Of this condition, 'I saw clearly,' wrote the painter of clowns, Rouault, 'that the "clown" was myself, ourselves, almost all of us.'[7]

The assignment of the part breaks the anticipated storyline for someone, in this instance a person already embarked upon a spiritual journey. It introduces a pause, provides a situation and distance from which one can look both ways, backward and forward, with regret and anticipation. But the theatre of the soul neither labels nor assigns judgements. Instead, it deepens sacred drama. Here are improvised the most telling of our personal rituals.

We have circumscribed our creative freedom to choose between different sacred faces of being by insisting upon belief in only one as defined by a specific religion or else we deny the existence of any sacred face at all by defining ourselves as secular or scientific. The archetypal dramas which shape the sacred face of such people prevent them from recognizing the patterning forces that underlie and shape the data they can recognize and the realities they cannot see. Dreams remind us that we need to honour our sacred face, not simply to yield to it but critically and creatively to understand and express or reject its fundamental force.[8]

Ritual is a form of behaviour resorted to when one is confronted with an enigmatic majesty and power beyond human apprehension. That force is felt to be numinous, unfathomable and overpowering but in the theatre of the soul its power is mediated and somehow balanced. It still remains awesome but its force is translated to human proportion and rendered capable of cognition.

In this connection Jung spoke of the compensatory rather than the corrective function of psyche itself, a function which brings unconscious contents to the surface at a rate and in a manner that makes it possible for them to be comprehended and assimilated.[9] Still, the process begins with a sharp, surprising summons from which one instinctively withdraws, feeling unwilling and/or unready to face the challenge. Yet, repeated engagements of this kind breed confidence and engender trust which is more durable than blind faith for one meets the adversary with one's eyes open and on symbolic ground. A mutual relationship is fostered and valued for which rite prepares the way in anticipation of thought.

Nevertheless, for this to happen, one's god has first to gain access to the soul. However ugly or threatening that figure may first appear – for example, 'the man in charge' – until it is acknowledged, the uncreated substance of all being is a common and diffuse energy without conscious hypostasis or shape, crude and ungainly, not unlike the clown. This character who is all of us but not any one of us, undeclared and uncommitted, beyond the bounds of accepted ego behaviour, hovers in the wings with freedom to express the inadmissible, say the unthinkable; arousing, revealing the opposites of feeling that lie hidden but not unfelt, possessing a power that can only be called magical to make one laugh or cry at the same time.[10] The lowest in the hierarchy, on the outermost edge of all orders and systems, without access to social mobility and devoid of psychic transformation, he or she embodies the fundamental unconscious wholeness of life, dependent upon impromptu responses reliant upon the impulse or whim of the moment.

True, the clown labours under the weight of all the emotions we will not or cannot make room for in lives focused upon the logical and predictable performances expected of us. So, archetypally he or she is a figure who plays out a shadow role in a sacrificial way, substituting for the ruling ego in rituals devised to atone for the ills of a given historic moment, circumstance or community. This figure is the primordial image of how the unclaimed self presents itself. The agony of the condition is real for the player. The white mask is a parody of individuality. Watching, we laugh in derision, observing a part-self mirror our inadequacy.

So, is it any wonder that a dream ego might resist playing the clown? It is only when we comprehend the role in its fullness that we can embrace both the challenge and something of its reward – the reward being that again it inevitably constellates empathy so that members of the audience see themselves as not unlike the actor, acknowledging, 'There too go I.'

Aware of this, one need no longer feel as alone in one's solitude. This too is a gift of the living theatre of the soul. It shows us what we are, what we may become, and, to some extent, its effect upon others. It presents us that which cannot be avoided but it does so while containing us in a private act with universal dimensions. Alone, one doesn't live. In the theatre of the soul the individual acting for himself or herself, discovers he or she acts also with and for a community.

'I have been on a train travelling north along with three other people,' a young priest dreams, 'I realize from a look at the foliage that it is an in-between season, neither summer or winter – maybe spring, maybe autumn. We get out at a remote station. Laughing good-naturedly, my companions and I climb a small hill on which I have some difficulty finding firm foot-holds but, reaching the top, we are able to look down on the sands and sea.

We watch two men who come riding from far inland to the shore. At the sea's edge they part and one rides directly into the water. The other dismounts and a young boy steps forward to take his horse. I can see the rider clearly and shout, "It's the Green Knight." His armour is green; his horse is caparisoned in green, glossy and sleek. In his left hand he holds a net and in his right a short lance, a sceptre perhaps or an axe? I dash down to meet him.

Time changes. My companions are now old men. I run swiftly along the beach, meet and pass two burly warriors coming from the other direction, men unshaven, stalwart and strong, bearded like Vikings, wearing the battledress of centuries past. I hasten on towards the knight who is waiting for me and watching. I find he is not old but older in time than any of us.'

With receipt of such a dream how can we regard psyche's stage as other than a theatre of sacred liminality? When it was still part of religion, theatre liberated the spiritual energy of an assemblage by incorporating myth, venerating, even profaning and transcending it. The audience along with the actors 'thus had a renewed awareness of personal truth in the truth of the myth portrayed and, through fright and a sense of the sacred, came to catharsis.'[11] This dream returns us to a concrete mythical situation, an experience of a common truth. 'It is the Green Knight,' the dreamer shouts. He dashes to meet him. Immediately, life's daily rhythm changes; it assumes the pace of the eternal; something occurs at the borders of human experience, a cathartic and historic interchange.

With the introduction of the myth we touch the encultured borderland of the sacred. Myths are recognized as stories that are treated as sacred or were once regarded as sacred. And they remain sacred inasmuch as they convey an otherworldly presence just as any archetypal vision does, but with a difference. They reveal that presence to ourselves and as ourselves, having the inherent power to change ourselves not through knowing but as being. So did the mime in the dream previously reported; so did the clown, but to admit this required an act of faith. However, the mythic presence already has a passport to belief through known connections. It can provide collective and historic references still circulating in the cultural consciousness of today.

Because of this there are psychotherapists who might question the alacrity with which a dreamer goes forward to meet the figure of the Green Knight, associated as he is with the challenge of death, a force which brooks no delay, seems not to care for personal priorities and despite everything, remains imperturbable, unalterable. The talent of the dream is that it introduces the figure, brings him on stage, gives him a form and portrays him just as he is, demanding as he has always done that he be met on his own terms. To the dreamer he no longer remains a spectre unseen; he is revealed, revealed consciously, while his herald and groom rides forward into the unconscious.

It was Aeschylus who first felt the necessity to bring the intrepid Furies on stage in flesh and blood. Commenting on this drastic change in Greek theatre, Jane Harrison remarked that Homer whose life preceded that of Aeschylus had no embodied shape for the eternal Angry Ones. He knew full well what they did, she said, but not how they looked; yet Aeschylus could no longer allow himself such vagaries. 'Up to the time when Aeschylus brought them on stage no one, if he had been asked what an Erinyes was like could have given any definite answer; they were unseen horrors that had never crystallized into set form.'[12]

In this dream, then, two things happen; the symbol is presented as myth and the myth, taking form, becomes image. It is placed in a specific location (on the edge of the sea), acquires a specific tone (the colour green), the Knight is given specific regalia (the horse, the net, the lance, the axe), a sex and age similar to the dreamer's own. All these things must be taken into account when interpreting productions played out in the inner theatre. They contribute to the lasting inwardness and impress of the drama. Without moralizing they foster a personal and responsive attitude. The performance is from fact to metaphor and the spectator/ actor has a renewed awareness of personal truth in the truth of the myth. Their inspiration, therefore, is only a point of embarkation, as it were. Their greatest lesson is one that must be discovered and integrated by oneself.

Is the dream, then, a psychological happening to be complemented and completed by religion – the encouragement of a religious attitude, a discovery of meaning? Or, is it not implicitly recognizable as religious in and of itself, with something incomparably intimate and transformative in the encounter when the god-likeness of the Green Knight is found portrayed in the dreamer's own psyche? This appears to be neither instruction nor preparation but revelation.

The dreamer is utterly exposed to the presence of the dream. We see here that what is spoken of as the transcendent function is an actual experience of the real and the imaginary (which is a psychological way of putting it), of both the human and the divine as one (which is a religious way of expressing it). Whichever reading is given depends upon the observer but in the instant of the dream they are inseparable to the one who dreams.

Whenever I teach or write, I am hesitant to use dreams except in an illustrative way. No-one can read from them the full story of any dreamer yet listeners or readers cannot help but make self-comparisons. Similarly I dislike epithets such as 'a typical Freudian dream' or to have one labelled as typically 'Jungian'. Such comments never do justice to the subjectivity of the dream itself.

Persons I work with dream about many things, of course, everyday happenings and commonplace events, but, just as their dreams have a psycho/personal content, they also have a psycho/sacred content as well. It is not by way of definition or classification that we know them but by their precise intrinsic contact which, like an arrow meeting its mark, shows the theatre of the soul to be a many splendoured hall for private viewings. And some do not point to ritual; they are, as is this one, implicitly, ritual enactments.

The danger with a dream such as the one of the Green Knight is, of course, that the more persuasive, fascinating and powerful the root metaphor is, the more chance it has of becoming part of a self-certifying personal myth. Psychotherapy, like ritual, goes awry when there is literal and unquestioning adherence to dream messages. A heavy responsibility is placed on a companion, therapist or priest to remain aware of the dynamics at work both in the dream and in his or her own choice of a myth of meaning with which to mediate response. Rather than reflecting a personal attitude, attempting to proselytize or regarding either a religious or psychological explanation as capable of substituting for the other, respect must be shown to the suggestion of an implicate order in the dream that transcends either one. Here two metaphors are active together and life is engendered by their coactivity.[13] Like mediumistic statements of all ages, the dream is sufficiently cryptic not only to leave the way open for interpretation but to require it.

What does the dream drama make possible? First, it provides a reciprocal encounter and a mythic enactment in some form. So long as the figure of the Green Knight, image of archetype or god, is kept at a distance and regarded as a remote and possibly threatening figure, the dreamer can concentrate energies upon avoidance. Perhaps he will assume his heroism is equal to or more than equal to the challenge of the meeting. But now it seems the delayed and destined time for confrontation has come.

Contact is established with the courier of death. This is not merely an intellectual meeting but one which involves oneself directly and totally, beginning with one's instinctive and unconscious reactions but eventually touching to one's most lucid and conscious choices. Perceptual reality of the presence is reinforced. 'How come? What for?,' the dreamer asks. 'What part am I supposed to play? How can I achieve a perspective in relation to the plot that will enable me to be creative? Is there a way to avoid anxiety but, if I do avoid it, won't that involve an avoidance of life as well?'

As companion to the dreamer at this stage on his soul's journey, the meaning that I, the therapist, attach to the incident will also influence the dreamer's attitudes. So this also enters the conscious environment of the dreamer and has a bearing upon a sacred/ human truth mutually and subjectively perceived. Interestingly, in the myth itself the point of the Knight's appearance is temptation and challenge so that the chosen youth gains by way of the mystery of death's intervention the treasure of everlasting life.[14] Consciousness is born out of the awareness of limitation.

The intimate intensity of a mutual exposure to something which reveals by violating a previous integrity of belief returns us to a concrete mythical situation. Thereby we become witnesses to and conscious participants in the founding of a myth of personal significance. For meaning does not emerge as an afterthought

from the act; in all rites it is inherent in the act itself. Only
another myth unconsciously active in our living assumptions can
function as a preventive and taboo. Defiance of that existing
taboo characterizes the struggle with a now newly perceived truth
by introducing a process in which what was once opaque in
someone slowly becomes transparent.

The full experience of that process, of course, is spoken of
differently in psychology than it is in the theatre and in the
world's religions where it is referred to as 'mystical enlightenment'. However, the labour is the same; it is to accept the challenge, as did Gawain, to venture, to select and use one's individual
possibilities unashamedly and to the utmost. The text is not our
concern here; the text emerges with the play. Still, there must be
a text. Without it the human drama becomes a series of shapeless
meanderings. Even the mime show has a theme.

The interpretation of our shifting roles as spectator, actor and
quasi-director must be left to each of us in command of the
talent, properties, preparation, conditioning and whatever other
resources we can muster. I sometimes wonder whether there is
anything else that can be hoped for in psychotherapy than a
freeing of such psychic resources as the ability to see (which very
old scriptural sources suggest is the same as to have or to possess),
to hear, to intuit, to feel, to respond – in fact, to use our entire
persons to perceive an inner summons and to relate fully to what
comes in the freedom of that knowledge.

If such attention is given to personal artistry I am quite sure
both actors and audience undergo changes and what we speak of
as maturity in performers in fact unfolds. One's own myth
of meaning is revealed through repeated enactments in which
the limits of one's power and that of a supraordinate force are
differentiated. Thereby, the form of one's humanity becomes
defined while that of the divine is engaged with and a reciprocal
relationship fostered. Inner theatre is sacred theatre. There scattered, accidental feelings and vague religious sentiments are
assembled and transformed into individual consciousness. 'The
seat of faith, however, is not consciousness but spontaneous
religious experience, which brings the individual's faith into
immediate relation with God.'[15] We can remember that the root
of 'spontaneous' is *spen* which is 'to draw across', 'to stretch', 'to
spin'.

Once a woman presented a dream which she had dreamed on

a still and quiet night, a night she described as being 'so still that you could have heard a feather fall'. In that dream she heard a wind rising as if at the onset of a storm. Startled from sleep, she roused herself with the intention of closing the shutters and windows of her house but to her surprise the night outside remained calm and quiet. Puzzled, she lapsed into sleep again and the dream continued with a voice saying, 'The wind that blows, blows in your own soul.' The words left a lasting impress and introduced her to a new perspective on life and her role in its significance.

We are actors who at times forget we play a part in what we are enacting. But then a rupture manifests that seems to cleave apart that so human view. The self that desires simply to be left alone and allowed to 'get on with it' breaks away from the self which senses that the drama of existence is of worth and that creation is a combined sacred and human venture. If one views it otherwise the main actor is imprisoned with his illusions and never allowed to participate creatively. Sadly, in this instance he or she never becomes a person.

The healing of the split lies in apprehending our condition as a mystery which it is impossible to express solely in human phrases and concepts since humanity itself partakes of that mystery. Humanity and mystery go together though neither is reducible to the other. The most necessary thing to retain in consciousness is that the drama is one that is a divine/human drama; it cannot be one-sidedly one or the other. That knowledge is matched by the psychological awareness that no script simply falls into a life from outside and no actor is assigned a role devoid of meaning.

With this insight the personal self can then reunite with the archetypal self and what is spoken of as personhood comes into being. An integrated person faces and receives knowledge of insight. There is a different comprehension of who one is and what one's place is in the world. There is an agreeable trust in reciprocity and one feels it is time to undertake something with respect to the sacred and that he or she may no longer live in disregard of it.

When Pirandello's *Six Characters In Search Of An Author* appear in a rehearsal room and successfully interrupt work in progress, the question is put to them by a frustrated producer:

'What exactly do you want to do? We don't make up plays here! We only present comedies and tragedies here.'

To this the father among the characters answers: 'That's right; we know that of course. That's why we've come.'

The producer then insists: 'And where's the script?'

The father replies: 'It's *in us*, sir. The play is in us: we *are* the play and we are impatient to show it to you. You see, we've been neglected.'[16]

Every individual performance risks an act of faith since it is not an illusion; it is a reality. Like Pirandello's *Six Characters In Search Of An Author* we are the characters and in the theatre of the soul live an act of faith which is an unveiling of things seen or a collecting of our part-selves to turn in the direction of the creative value. The myth we observe forms the basis or framework for the experience of entire generations but it is for us to re-enact it conscious of its transformative potential. This involves a sense of identity, direction, timing and will, requiring all our energies to translate the truth as we witness it. Thereafter, like prophets we convey new meanings. In genuine prophecy the Source and the Prophet are one.

Personality takes shape on the stage of an inner theatre. The actions flow from an inner necessity. They are not simply messages transmitted from elsewhere, however much they appear to be so at times but they spring quite as much from a *principium individuationis* which draws a person towards these unknowns so that he or she finds and tests the obstacles which stand in the way of being one's self. If that self calls forth a priest they take one form but those with religious vocations are not the only people to be presented with sacred images.

A contemporary and highly able man but someone who would consider his deskwork most mundane dreams:

'I am living at St John's with my wife and family. I go to an outbuilding which is on the grounds but a long way from the house. It is a chapel. Inside I find chippings and pieces of stone discarded by a stonemason.

I pick out one piece which I like. The one I choose is a rectangular piece of polished marble and on its surface is an architect's design of a church. It is different from all the others which are sandstone.

It's heavy. I just manage to pick up my stone and stagger

with it towards the main house. The easiest way home is along the river bed. I have to walk through the water carrying my block of marble. It immediately becomes light and manageable once I am in the water but the weight will make it difficult to get out onto the path to the house.'

A dream fascinates us. It attracts attention and from ancient times to the present day many kinds of approaches have been used for interpretation. One of the most seductive is to interpret on the basis of a predefined imagery in the hope that this will spur a reluctant ego to complete its task. But isn't this technique similar to that used by a clergyperson who might undertake to translate scripture allegorically? It conveys an evaluative, corrective and essentially intellectual message in contrast to the approach of the dream itself or the attitude of psyche. This is an attitude that invites us to notice, to listen and respond feelingly, attentive to a summons that offers more than its gestures suggest immediately and encourages the assumption that it, the dream, needs us as much as we need it.

Theoretically, psyche's view infers that the self is integral rather than opposed to the rest of the personality and its function is to work in conjunction with an ego prepared to listen, to love, and, yes, as in this instance willing to sweat for it. The dream speaks metaphorically. Stripping away personal encumbrances, it mythologizes yet it speaks directly as one does to an individual for whom a message is intended and as if the message could be heard. 'There is a telling moment of impact when this recognition strikes and one is held as by the mystery of one's own face in a glass.'[17]

The mirror to which the dreamer of the foregoing dream is held is not one in which he can easily recognize himself or he might say that the dream may reveal a hidden intuitive urge though not one he would dare expose to the outer world. It doesn't surprise him that psyche locates the dream at St John's for that is where his family once lived in a house built on the site of an early but now ruined monastery. Yet, it has been years since he moved away from St John's and, of course, there was no chapel on the property.

That he should find there among fragments left by a stonemason a piece of marble is also surprising since marble was not an indigenous stone and would have had to be imported. Yet he chooses this unlikely piece incised with the design of a church and is ready to try and get it back to the main house. Quite alone, he carries it to the river and undertakes a solitary journey through the water which suggests a kind of cleansing or baptism. 'It felt good to do it,' he says, 'but if that's surprising to me, think how surprised others would be if they knew what I did.'

We are actors, perhaps like the dreamer, who at times are less than fully mindful of the parts we play in relation to what we are addressing. We attend to obvious roles expecting to fulfil social and traditional expectations while at the same time assuming that these connect us with the thread of our authentic persons. And, as individual actors, we move through patterned sequences with others while at the same time presuming that we are making choices.

These assumptions about form and custom make special demands on our behaviour, govern assessments of our perform-ances and desires, permit some and reject others automatically. Nevertheless, concurrently our dreams will suggest rather differ-ent and life-enhancing alternatives that lie just below the surface of consciousness. These latent possibilities can be secretly enjoyed or disdained, welcomed or discarded but even so will remain somewhere on the periphery of choice even though repressed and denied integration with our subjective natures.

However, the theatre of the soul is by nature a theatre wherein mystery is acknowledged and portrayed as fact. The recognition and safeguarding of its ritual aspect are ultimately a safeguarding of the human person as well and the possibility of that person's experiencing its complete and individual nature. The dream message conveys an inarticulate and unborn Word which is ready to enter subjectivity and be made incarnate. Work upon the dream, 'befriending it', will involve the transposition of such objective and unintelligible speech into subjective and compre-hensible terms while at the same time preserving the potency of its utterance and prophecy.

The play itself takes place astride what Paul Claudel spoke of as 'the two sides of a book – the visible and the invisible, the real and the surreal, the physical and the metaphysical, the flesh and the spirit'.[18] If we speak of a masterful performance by an actor we refer to a performance given with a sense of both. And it will be a subjective performance arising from the entire person as opposed to the alternative of a performance limited by objective circumstances alone.

The performance arrests us, then seems holy because it expresses holiness, though not in a way that can be attributed to any catechism or judged by a single morality. That is, it naturally and implicitly acknowledges a combined production springing from a divine/human source. When in search of solutions we often neglect to acknowledge that source, but psyche does not. It behaves as if it existed.

Chapter 4

The rite of creativity

That which is creative must create itself.
Keats

For her the labour of the shields was a ritual undertaking; it opened the way to a new depth of realization both for psyche and for person. In retrospect, the weaver became aware that she alone could not have been responsible for the inspiration; her weaving had been undertaken in response to an inner summons and the anticipation of these pieces had extended over many years. The work served both to separate and unite two parts of her life. After she left the looms she was certain of that and was more settled for the creative impulse had become a burning necessity. What she did was spoken of as ageless and transcendent even though it was composed of basic and elemental materials, old and new. To conceive it had been a celebration.

They were called The Shields of the Amazons and reinterpreted an age-old story. From them could be read the mystery of woman's life and defences. They were the colour of blood, the earth and the forest, the sea and the night. Seeing them one was strangely moved, feeling disturbed and empowered at the same time. They seemed more than the stuff of which they were woven. They were of the stuff from which myths are made.

It was not I who said it. At the top of the stairs, facing the loft where the pieces were exhibited, with her first glimpse of the shields my companion spoke half aloud as if to herself, 'She has made sacred objects.' I agreed.

In the experience of our work we had been schooled to the knowledge that an individual is someone who inevitably belongs to two worlds simultaneously. A person, that is, cannot be adapted solely to a social and cultural world but is always moving beyond the boundaries of that world, focusing attention on a synthesis evidenced by creative acts that embody both personal fullness and freedom. Without that impetus, we would agree, one found no evidence of creative power.

An individual belongs to two worlds. One world alone does not afford sufficient satisfaction and the creative act derives from both. 'It is the entire person who receives and interprets inspiration in wholeness – not abstract, partial and merely psychological man or woman.'[1] Such perceptions, I realize, concern the involvement of someone in an act that is essentially ritualistic. If that act belongs to an artist, it is no less valid for an analyst, an actor, a believer or priest. It adheres to the profession of our professions. Without it ritual, art and personhood do not exist. It is here that the symbolic relationships between the two worlds have their existence.

In the theatre of the soul, consciously or otherwise, the role of destiny is assigned to the Sacred. This is a theme which has given birth to countless dogmatic variations. Yet, when truth is received it is not a collection, even a private collection, of abstract principles. It is perceived as a sharp feathered word and the word is about ourselves; we are its subject. It appears as the result of a collaboration in which creation is activated. Person and Meaning meet and a new organon or system of thought is born of the meeting.

With the possibility of creation a different factor is introduced into one's natural everyday existence, a factor that appears to be the essence and primal ground of all things though it cannot be described phenomenally. It is on offer, so as to speak, but to reach it asks for an exercise of courageous choice. A point of contact is made with a destiny validated within (i.e. psychologically) as well as identifiable as the goal towards which the human person inclines (i.e. religiously).[2] The meeting with destiny involves one with a rite of claiming the relationship called creativity and leads to personhood. It introduces a process termed individuation by analytical psychologists.

Yet, paradoxically the free creative act operates in an environment of darkness and meets with resistance from personal necessity. This is not a condition but becomes an activity in which to quote one of the giants of theatre, 'what is dark in us slowly becomes transparent'. It cannot be otherwise.

And, though what is activated becomes capable of taking infinite and varied form, it is apprehended precisely by virtue of its relationship to personal revelation while that which we experience as revealed brings with it an imperative, is transformative, becomes precious, requires expression and bears the seed of further revelation. Something formerly known by its connection with shadow, mystery and darkness takes on a new guise in relation to identity and imagination. Thereafter a thing, a place, a time, a circumstance or fellow human with these attributes we will recognize as out-of-the-ordinary and accord it the highest value. How can we describe this 'something' if not as the fundamental, archetypal source of life and speak of it as the Sacred?

Afterwards one can then say of being, as Taoist painters did of their work, that negative space is pregnant there; fulsome, the production contains more than is yet apparent in itself.[3] With this awareness, the artist of life will then work 'from the inside out', from the centre of the composition towards its outreach and completion, so as to speak, whatever materials are given. But to do so, as one of the early Taoist masters wrote, it is necessary that 'a painter accumulate his power until he arrives at the stage when he can rely on himself as possessing the bamboo (or other subject of his painting) – possessing it completely in *himself*'.[4]

For this to be possible Taoists assumed that the creativity of the artist was itself linked with a natural principle, that which they spoke of as spirit resonance or the inborn capacity to imaginatively complete a given design in harmony with its fundamental urge. Furthermore, since it was assumed to be instinctive and natural, they supposed that this same resonance was available to viewers as well. Here there are intimations of our present-day concept of a natural self awaiting dedicated and imaginative completion in the personality. The work of the artist, then, is to communicate the fundamental urge without prefiguring its form. Hence, an artist is defined as someone who, in possession of life, both conscious and unconscious, produces forms that activate spirit resonance in others.

Sustained, disciplined ritual preparation was considered necessary in order to assist the spiritual realization of the Taoist artist. Only after the most profound and subtle cleansing was it felt that the painter could receive creative enlightenment. Then as now, artistic and spiritual rites demand disciplined readiness in anticipation of realization or enlightenment of some kind. A heightened awareness is fostered, concentrated upon the ripening of a soul's intuition so that it is open to receive and transmit, as if effortlessly, that which is awakened and revealed. Now as then, within those who are entrusted with receipt and transmission of spirit resonance – actors, artists, priests, all must be moulded to that end; mediation of that quality becomes their profession and vocation.

That is to say the one who is a mediator of spirit resonance guides the Sacred and his or her role is different from other ritual participants, partakers or parishioners. The latter are receivers, members of an audience responsible only for awareness of their personal orientation while the priests, the artists, and the actors mediate from the perspective of the infinite creator.[5] To do that asks for sensitivity to messages born of two desires. The actor, artist or priest stands at a midpoint of movement and yearning, the yearning and movement of a person towards experience of the supraordinate and divine and that of the Sacred towards person.

To see what one transmits as from the sacred side of being one must acknowledge it, trust it and be ready to 'speak' on its behalf, to have the courage to interact with it and, finally, to be faithful and responsible to it. In a sense, these are holy persons. Like Taoist painters they unite with the primal stuff of the medium with which they work.[6] Yet, the role of mediator has its own discipline; to fulfil it they cannot become other than themselves, human beings within whom the image of a sacred source has ripened as the result of a creative and conscious relationship to their own fundamental selves. Otherwise, they would be charlatans and sorcerers, falling prey to an invasion of creative power.

We all know that present-day as well as ancient observances have, nevertheless, included practices that are cruel and damaging. Whatever is the expressed intent of such practices, they are noticeably flawed by an abuse of creative power. Rites are fostered that become one-sidedly biased and the opposite of creative exchange.

The communal symbol has power to draw out suppressed and unconscious collective insights and a mediator who is possessed by the shadow of authority and power will let go of human restraint giving way to emotional excess. An inundation of archetypal energies results and produces an inflated condition not unknown in the theatre and referred to as 'going over the top'. When this happens, the mediator then, like the unfortunate actor,

loses awareness of himself or herself and identifies with the role
of the initial Creator. Enactment becomes an acting-out. What
transpires is no longer transformative; it becomes a tragic and
senseless ordeal. Human life inflated by a sense of sacred power
and invested with rites can be absolutely and entirely stifled by
them.

This being a temptation, how can the shock, fear and wonder
generated by the numinous experience of transformation be
mediated appropriately? It is impossible, even unwise, to try and
eliminate such reactions for they are essential to the interaction
of the forces involved. But the rites need to be practised with
regard for their symbolic and metaphorical import in ways that
neither inhibit nor block the freedom and enterprise of participants.

The working through of such susceptibilities is the core of
initiation and yields one of the most profound gifts of any ritual
process; namely, the discovery that individual freedom means
responsibility to no other authority than the creative power
through which one gives an answer to the divine appeal. 'Any
genuine symbol, with its accompanying ceremonial rite becomes
a mirror that reflects new insights, new possibilities, new wisdom,
and other psychological and spiritual phenomena that we do not
(yet) dare experience on our own.'[7] Humility and a sense of
proportion need to be fostered to supplant the likelihood of a
seduction to transcendence of human limitations. Regard for this
will have to do with the timing, the pace, the gestures and the
costuming, the script and its rhythms – in other words, attunement
of a universal theme to human proportion for all, all will be
symbolically received by the open soul at that time.

There are ritual observances, both traditional and modern, that
foster this kind of awareness while at the same time they appear
to transcend their visible form, themselves becoming transcen-
dently metaphorical. These rites are both containers of symbols
and symbol-makers, partially though never fully lifting the veil of
mystery and obscurity which envelop the unknown. They offer
an abundance of opportunities for amplification of insight with
direct personal relevance while directives are kept to a minimum.
Yet, as a result the careful observer or initiate notes an astonishing accuracy of revelations which match but do not exceed human
and individual possibilities, which challenge but do not damage
self-worth.

The structure of such rituals never becomes outmoded. Their vitality does not diminish. Though they may be neglected for long periods, forgotten, discarded or otherwise repressed, they lie fallow in the collective unconscious until time is ripe for their renewal. It is these that spontaneous rites most often duplicate without rehearsal or teaching. Their messages anticipate a breakthrough of the numenal world into phenomenal existence and they are witnessed with an attitude of expectancy and awe as if the sacred source of being were standing in the wings incognito, awaiting a cue to be brought on stage.

The ability to transcend form or become translucent with meaning – isn't this the same quality that distinguishes a great and lasting work of art as well; a painting, the design of a cathedral, a poem, a drama, a piece of music or perhaps the weaving of a fibre artist? To the onlooker the work becomes fertile with renewing possibilities and it is this which intermediaries are there to protect. Likewise, is it not necessary to acknowledge that transitional rites will inevitably expose the themes of dread, suffering and transformation? Mediation of these motifs is their purpose, their *raison d'être*.

We are used to speaking of art as creative, though less often do we speak about ritual in a similar manner. Certainly, genuine art in contrast to contrived art is creative; the artist evidences an application of primary freedom to interact with the ultimate mystery, an application which coincides with a personal necessity to reveal the undisclosed. But not all that is called art is creative any more than all rite, drama or otherwise. Yet, each retains the potential of revelation and disclosure when met subjectively and respected as living symbol. '*Someone*,' writes Olga Sedakova, one of the most inward-looking of Russia's young poets, '*Someone* is looking at a painting that is locked in a storeroom, someone who appeared with that painting.'[8]

Likewise, Jacqueline Morreau writes,

> I believe that all human beings are linked to each other, and therefore are capable of understanding each other's symbols and works of art. Not that they always do, but they *can*. The artist is someone who out of her or his life, both conscious and inner, produces symbolic forms which can have meaning for others.[9]

With the renewed interest and fascination for symbol that characterize late twentieth-century life we are tempted to insert symbolic forms into expression of our arts. But symbols discretely evade conscious selection and application, just as the woven Shields of the Amazons could not have been intended for ritual use. Instead, the making of them was a ritual undertaking, a re-enactment of creation in a unique and individual form that united symbol and Source for the artist. Seeing them, by way of their innate symbolism a way is prepared for the viewer to take his or her own journey towards sacred awareness.

For a work of art is capable of stimulating a mythic response, standing as it does midway between role and being. Symbols expressed in their verity introduce us to myth but also nourish the transgression of its literal and obvious message. A myth taken literally and acted out can no longer fulfil that function. It loses its figurative and transitional quality, no longer carrying the seed of a hidden and further truth. In their purity the myth, the dream, meditation, the parable and the liturgical canon all remain open-ended to infinity yet bring it closer to the here and now in ourselves.

At a time when life becomes static and regeneration is not forthcoming, personal or collective renewal can be found only by confrontation with the images that attack the environment of the soul with power to block psychic movement and change. However fantastic or far-fetched these images appear to be, they are recognizable as part of a universal thesaurus of meanings of which the priest, the artist and the actor along with the analyst are poetic masters. The work of all four rests on a foundation of archetypal imagery and awareness of sacred sources along with an understanding that the symbols, like electrical connections, function as conductors of insight, energy and potential.

Anyone who attempts to work with ritual symbolism without reference to both an archetypal and a personal context is confronted with difficulties since the work will be cut off from its source as well as from the receiver. The wisdom of both religion and psychology indicates that ritual behaviour is resorted to because it provides sanctuary and ultimate security for the condition of souls besieged and is intuitively recognized to be of the highest value since it validates and gives meaning to the anxious frustrations of personal living. So here an intepreter who tries to work solely from an objective point of view invades an area related to what is considered most private, guarded and precious by the human person. Intrusions will be met with resistance and resentment.

The subjective expectations of ritual experience and trust are frequently projected onto analysis and analysts even though such effects are not intentionally products of analysis. Rather, they are discoverable in the place where analysis does not consciously go. They adhere instead to images of the infinite and a relationship to the sacred element of being. Only by chance do they emerge from the logic of everyday life experience. Rather they have to do with how one approaches the presence of the divine image one carries, how it is met, how its word is communicated and finally how someone relates to that word. Undoubtedly analysis touches upon these things and at times analysts will unwittingly stumble across sanctified boundaries. We expose, perhaps, but we must never invade or discredit for we cannot offer a substitute.

Once when lecturing on Jungian concepts to a group of counsellors in training I had in my class a handsome young Negro who had grown up in the Deep South of the United States. He then seemed somewhat of an outsider on the London scene. Throughout our lectures and discussions, though attentive, he remained quiet and withdrawn. For several weeks he was silent until at last a day came when he shared with us a telling insight.

That morning my subject was the archetype of the shadow and as I proceeded, I observed that this man was becoming more and more restless, as if perhaps awakening from a long sleep. When I reached the point of explaining that the Shadow contains not only the detritus of life but also the potential of the as yet unknown and unrealized self, it seemed he could hardly contain himself any longer. So I stopped and turned to him directly, saying, 'You look as if you want to speak.'

'Yes, I do,' he replied emphatically. 'Yes, I do!'

'What do you want to say?' I asked.

He then spoke impulsively and at length while the rest of us listened, somewhat astonished and spellbound.

'Now I understand!' he began. 'Now I understand what my mother meant!

'It was summer and it was hot. It was near noontime and we kids were out in the back yard playing "Catch One Another's Shadow" when my mother came to the door. She took one look around that yard and then she opened the door wide. "You kids come in here this very minute and you sit down in the kitchen, every one of you," she commanded.

'We filed in and we sat down. She was frowning like I'd never seen her. She pointed her finger straight at us and she said' – the young man's voice became tense with emotion; he was obviously roused by what he remembered – '. . . she said, "Don't you ever let me find you playing that game again! Just you remember a man's shadow is sacred and don't *you* ever try to take it away from him!" '

The lecture room was silent. The incident and the delivery of the young man's message left a strong impression. He was neither priest nor artist but he had affirmed for us a fundamental truth. An emotional memory long imprisoned in shadow had now unblocked a source of daring which opened the way for creativity to be expressed. He had spoken with his own voice. We could but acknowledge that his mother was right and he had understood.

A person's shadow is sacred; it is by way of it that we are able to face our dread, our shame and guilt with any hope of resti-tution, absolution and grace. For it is there that the potential of unclaimed personhood resides. There we find the hidden impulse that we experience as 'the flash of the fire that can',[10] an energy that allows us to emerge from whatever darkness may have over-taken us as someone changed and other than we were.

The arts themselves are products of differentiation. They orig-inated in the temple; they developed from an unconscious unity in which all parts were subject to a religious centre and, impor-tantly, they are capable of leading back to it. They alter time; they alter space and orientation. They foster awareness and give birth to a new kind of joy.

To enable and consecrate this passage all authentic rituals have been devised. For this reason too they are fundamentally initiat-ory; by the creative act we are able to reach beyond a seeming death. Immobile and empty, while at the same time longing to find a word relevant to our dark and seemingly godless condition we approach them prepared to surrender or sacrifice something of a previous identity even without evidence of hope for finding more. So doing, whether or not we ever enter a church, a temple, a synagogue, a mosque or other sanctified place, we discover not that we are one with the gods but that something of the gods takes up residence in us and can be called by our name.

A point of ultimate orientation is reached in conditions that are instantaneous and contemporary. To waken to this realization is a shock, as the young man in the lecture room and all who have felt it might attest. Contrary to what is popularly believed, creative artists, saints and heroes fight the actual rather than the ideal gods of our society – the god of conformism, for example, as well as the gods of apathy, greed and power. Henceforth and thereafter an enlightened one is consciously entrusted with the art and process of his or her own life; having been shown the natural creativity of the universe revealed in specific and personal terms.

This is to say that our most profound insights come to us by surprise and arise out of human conditions and circumstances. Life-altering revelations are not often vouchsafed in the form of dissociated visions; neither are they readily discernible from the study of exotic texts. They cannot be sought after consciously. Instead, in the midst of difficult and commonplace tensions an impact is made by receipt of a palpable and unforgettable intuition which penetrates to the heart of the situation and transforms it.

The impress of such an insight is stamped on the soul forever and creates sacred history for a person. Yet, over generations we have been conditioned to reject the notion that a divine aspect is characteristic of our human nature and pervades it. So the realization is accompanied by a haunting strangeness that asks for verification, and we later seek, by way of whatever mentors and mediators we dare trust, wisdom and acceptance of that truth. Finding the solitary responsibility for infinite revelation too great to bear, we search for a community of witnesses and a form of celebration to affirm and contain us while we attempt to absorb transcendence.

These are notions, however, that will be eschewed by psychologists who labour to explain the self with the logic of the mind rather than the innate logic of psyche. What psyche appears to yearn for at a time of supreme challenge and breakthrough is no longer an objective god. It reaches towards and accepts one ready to become subjective. And yet, the phenomenal experience is intimidating.

Theoretical considerations are left behind, at least temporarily. The evident need is for time, care and empathy to be directed to the transcription of what is now a private and individual intelligence derived from a universal reservoir of spiritual truths. For unless the insight can be understandingly shared and validated in the presence of at least one other companion it stagnates, eventually becomes encapsulated and destructive. If lived, however, being accorded respect and place as part of an ongoing story – all stories but also my story – it retains the possibility of being transformed and recycled again and again.

As we have already been made aware, to be alone is to die as an individual. In the sequence I reported in Chapter One, André had not yet become an individual recognizable to himself psychologically. Existing as a fugitive, his psyche isolated and estranged, how could he hope to find a home for an imagined self except in altered states, artificially induced? What he actually sought in his psychic wanderings was sanctuary for soul. This was his primary need, sanctuary and affirmation of his own existence.

In sanctuary aloneness and terror abate; communion and security are assured. Temporarily or otherwise, rituals offer sanctuary for they cohere the flux of life and protect it. One can almost say that the acceptance of ritual is an attempt at reconciliation of the divine/human dichotomy. Neither family, church nor politics had provided sanctuary for André. In his frustration he and many others have turned to drugs, sex and art. The first reflects pathology; the latter possibility.

But no longer do we often associate art with sanctuary or link religion with artistry except if artists choose to represent religious subjects. Most artists speak of their calling as if it were simply demandingly hard work. They try to limit their comments to plausible and rational statements, being wary of sounding pedantic, arrogant or esoteric. But the value of art itself is not necessarily diminished by other and seemingly far-out interpretations. Associating it with the sacred reasserts a valid and ancient connection, tested historically and universally. The state of the artist who actively waits, alert to the unformed vision, is a state of readiness comparable to prayer, and by analogy the studio, no different from the sacred cell of a monk, can be a place set apart where one undergoes a creative inner process of anticipation, suffering, breakthrough and faith.

The *temenos* established in the analytic consulting room also provides secluded space within which it is possible to observe the constellation of the individual self. But, unlike a person who approaches analysis, the believer who is fully dedicated to a ritual life or the serious artist has already made the essential choice to pursue the real self or understanding of the inner state of things as they are in their essence. Neither is in pursuit only of an experimental or aesthetic goal but one that is essentially religious. An inherent philosophy informs it, a philosophy which, combined with motivation and supported by technique, is capable of producing a unique and individual result.

An inner urge prompts the encounter with art, whether or not it can be explicitly traced. A melodic theme, a scripture, a subtext, a hidden symmetry runs through it, runs parallel to the state of the artist's soul, uniting faith and expressed being while the function of disciplined practice is essential to realization of the image it inspires. The connection between inspiration and product seems to be grounded in a commitment that provides for creative intercourse between the impetus and the composition, between subject and object, a commitment which by nature is intuitively accessible to the god-thought. It is impossible to will either revelation or creativity but one can consciously offer oneself to the encounter with intensity of dedication and purpose.

Some artists accept their work is rite and those aware of the innate generative power of their religious vocations enact ritual as art. The difference between the two lies, on the one hand, with the aim of the artist to present art as being and, on the other, the purpose of the religious to perfect being as art. Their common material is the malleable substance of the human soul.

Certainly the calling of an artist demands hard, disciplined work and the doing of it also acts as a mode of release and renewal. All applied rites have significance when they provide us freedom to transcend our blinkered and stereotyped vision so that, in the act of relinquishing previous visions, we better discern who we are and are more able to entrust ourselves to something we cannot name though we sense indwells within us. Ritual undertakings offer seclusion and protection wherein the creative relationship of ourselves with the power of such an indwelling image is sensitized and fostered. The soul is safeguarded and given permission to experience its nature honestly and to the full.

By choosing to inhabit a solitary space we accept responsibility for becoming our own mediators of the self without form. In the sanctuary of the inner person works of art are forged. It becomes the *fundus animae* where the Sacred and the soul converge. What we then produce we have every right to call a total act, signifying as it does our human willingness to consciously relate our energies to the demands of the unrevealed called divine. The identity that is generated emphasizes the essential unity of the two and goes far deeper than the correspondence between something and its symbolic image. The one becomes the other.[11]

We now perceive that an act of creation has very little to do with external satisfaction or with simply 'letting go'. Art itself is neither descriptive of an elevated state nor does it pertain to the status of a person in the sense of a profession or performance of a social function. It has a more profound significance. For sanctuary provides an inviolate refuge. The one who invokes sanctuary is pursued no further and the refuge becomes a world in itself. There all that happens is ritualistic; two spirits that are identically sensitive sensitize one another.

Here is an illustration of the 'negative space' regarded as an essential of Taoist art, a place where spirit resonance assumes form as an image capable of embodying two desires. There is no longer a place for a god applying outward force; the force is one with its nature. Here we discover as well that the creative deed is ever and in some manner an act of faith for it involves a struggle to believe in and yield to that which is nascent but not yet become apparent.

The sage withdraws from the group and takes sanctuary in solitude believing that thereby he better serves the group. In solitude the soul prepares for enlightenment and the act performed in solitude is enacted for us all, ritually liberating the soul from the conditioning of civilization. In this way the hermit and the artist are reflections of one another as the Taoists knew. What the one does through prayer and meditation the other does by way of art, actualizing spirit or creative intuition in the form of the work.[12]

At the borders of mediation between ourselves and the divine Self we always *found* in the sense that we break with tradition and provide a new way of seeing the past. As they themselves submit to initiation by creation, artists fulfil themselves and as a consequence what they offer is capable of initiating others in turn. Attitudes roused by their images honour that purpose.

Artistry can be interpreted psychologically as a process of cleansing and liberation of 'the real self' from claims of 'the false self'. But this is accepted as defining the work of many psychotherapists as well. Rightly, it is integral to their theory and informs their practice. For a rite of creativity always involves the creation of something 'other' as a result of renouncing what we have previously claimed as genuine and sufficient.

And yet, the product is something more than we can reach by way of theoretical understanding, disciplined application or ascetic practice alone. It is a function of relationship to the spiritual resources upon which creative living depends. It appears to emerge from the concentration of creative insight, the ability to cherish that insight, respond to it and mould it. The art and mystery of creativity lie in the loving and attentive mediation of insight to its realization for creation is basically a process of making, of bringing to birth.[13]

Every creative artist submits to that which he or she is given while the results transform origins in a way that meaningfully transfigures life. When opened to view this happening will be perceived and interpreted differently by religious or artistic schools. Implicit, however, is the recognition that the rite of creativity grounds the god-thought in reality. The end product, one in itself, speaks of both the inspiration and the inspired.

Certainly there are also artists of genius who create without conscious thought or acknowledgement of 'the greater'. This way they become victims of their own unconscious impulses but that does not mean that their works are void of the sacred. They are, instead, its object, and, again, by the directness of their imagery they are able to amplify for us the nature both of the Creator and creation for their works speak of renewal.

The key to the reality of primal sacred experience, which itself is wholly inaccessible, is meaning, a personal meaning interwoven with the act of revealing itself. Individual revelations are connected with the holism of an essential nature and subsist there initially as unrealized images of the soul. The images have nothing in common with photographs yet they possess their own magnetism, their own importance, their own laws; and it is oneself as artist who is entrusted to intercede for them in the act of creative living whereby their value is cherished and made evident.

There is a connection here with the Shields of the Amazons that my friend and I saw exhibited. In a cultural environment vigorously assertive of feminism they were shown and interpreted as symbolic of woman's urgent struggle to protect herself from male supremacy but they were more than that. 'Naturally, the Amazons never actually existed,' writes René Malamud.[14] Still, we know that stories of Amazons have been recounted and expanded over time and elsewhere than in pre-Christian Greece. Such figures are of mythic dimension and speak of profound conditions of soul and being.

In what I have called the rite of creativity revelation transforms a personal myth of meaning into something other, more rich and substantial. The artist exercises a fundamental creative freedom to play an active role in an individual and perhaps a collective destiny by restoring renewal to nature. The choice to assume that place signals a readiness to submit to the art of allowing oneself to be transformed and thereby discovering what Taoists apprehended as spirit resonance and making it accessible to others.

Inspiration initiates a surprising and puzzling sequence. The ways in which creative energy are expressed in life are manifold and remarkable. Any of them can reach the point of art.[15] But it is one thing to observe an aesthetic or ritual process and wonder at its effects while it is quite another to reach an adequate understanding of what it implies inwardly and subjectively.[16] The fullness of human life is surely not realizable in the form of social functioning of people but in their inner, individual selves, their souls.

We return again to the loft where two women silently gaze at an artist's creation, sprung forth from a place beyond penetration by our limited and immediate vision. So different from what we customarily imagine, the art becomes a metaphor of the metaphysical. It belongs to an altogether different scheme of things from that we have previously called reality or conceived as religious. But my companion was right, I reflect. The artist has created sacred objects.

The image slowly recreates itself in me. While contemplating this creation I suddenly become aware in a flash of intuitive understanding that here is not only a composition of symbolic intelligence and artistry. It is also something which actually reveals and makes real the living spirit and essence of our nature and along with it the divinely human character that pervades it.

Unrealized creativity is the most valuable and characteristic trait of fundamental human being and it becomes apparent to me that like veils these objects shield that most precious and vulnerable substance, the uniqueness of inward vision which can so easily be transgressed. They shield and, at the same time, they disclose and open it to renewal in life. As a consequence their message transcends and transforms the literalism of their historic time.[17]

Chapter 5

Listening to subjectivity

Religious rituals and stories help us so to live that we find psychic fulfilment in creative and expressive action. That *is* the conquest of evil and despair.

Don Cupitt

The person who creates is a microcosm but the creative act embraces the cosmos for ends are not set from without; they are born of creative effort. The act of appraisal which must be made by someone if he or she is to resolve a situation that does violence to himself or herself and demands solution is associated with imagination. But the image that prompts it is linked with knowledge which is neither empirical nor rational.[1] And the response involves an ever more attentive listening, a listening that examines as it listens and before it responds.[2] ... a listening which is not a running away but whereby 'the silence is to be heard resounding ... and the world, the gods, person, and all things have only to be looked upon with a new eye'.[3]

These thoughts have been expressed by contemporary philosophers, one a theologian, and by a scholar of comparative culture and religion. But there is nothing here with which a Jungian analyst would disagree. Jung's psychology has asserted that the experiences through which we live are at the same time conscious and unconscious, psychological and religious, material and spiritual. In practice it maintains that with integration of the dichotomy symbolized by circumstance personal wholeness and balance are achieved.

It has acknowledged the presence of a supraordinate and ordering principle active in the personality from the outset. This force has been identified as one of the intrapsychic archetypes and called the self. In relationship with it we give expression to a sacred source of being. The symbol-making function of the psyche is accepted as transcendent to the purposes of the conscious ego and allows for a compensatory process to take place which balances and reconciles the demands of the two, the ego which is capable of consciousness and the archetypal, unrealized self.

Through ritualization it is possible for a third position to be achieved in the personality, a position which partakes of both ego presence and consciousness of self. This acts as a counterbalance to the mass-mindedness of the rational world while at the same time it represents the legitimate claims of an extramundane point of reference. In the person a *modus vivendi* is thereby attained and mutuality fostered between inner and outer demands. Such interplay provides the source of an effective moral and ethical position.[4]

This introduction states a thesis illustrated and amplified in this chapter. Here the statement has been condensed almost to formulaic proportions but there are surprisingly relevant applications evident in attempts to resolve the ethic of our time. My deepening awareness of this has been by way of a sequence of observations both personal and professional – some of them reasoned, some intuitive, but all of them deeply felt, experienced and concerned with the psychological relationship of ideas, imagination and personal morality.

For several years I have watched the dispersion of confused and alienated persons into New Age adventures and therapies. As witness to this migration of souls I have questioned why such people chose to forego traditional practices and I have tried to discern what they sought elsewhere. Some but not all of them have returned to holistic analysis and former relationships impatient, disheartened and disillusioned if not damaged.

With the information derived from contacts with such people and by further reflection upon the impact of our chaotic times, particularly upon young people, it would seem that the majority set forth initially in search of renewed relevance for living. This can be traced as the underlying though largely unconscious motivation in almost every case. Despite apparent sophistication and for all their trendy apparel, they seem to have set out upon their journeys with the guileless simplicity of Parsifal.

Here, as in an individual analysis, there are repeated and predictable indicators of a process of transformation at work, a social process more extensive and profound than was conscious to the persons involved and, unfortunately, largely inaccessible to their present-day social theorists. 'The calculating production of technology is an "act without an image",' Heidegger quotes.[5] He goes on to say:

> Purposeful self-assertion, with its designs, interposes before the intuitive image the project of a merely calculated product. . . . The sphere of the objectivity of objects remains inside consciousness. What is invisible to that which stands-over-against belongs to the interior and immanence of consciousness.[6]

The analyst immediately identifies that which 'stands-over-against' conscious perception as the subjective position of the unconscious.

Whatever else the shift of contemporary focus away from established expectations and practices has revealed, it has shown us, psychological practitioners of various kinds, two important areas of neglect. We have failed to include social behaviours as being within the scope and purview of psychological functioning,[7] nor have we often dared to apply our insights and techniques to collective problems.[8]

As a consequence, being loath to expand, extend or involve ourselves with society's problems and in relation to social issues, we have by and large ignored the relevance of our input. But we have also most often neglected to associate ourselves compassionately with others who are most concerned with problems disclosed to us daily, in depth, problems of relevance, religion and commitment.

What I attempt here is once again to bridge the gap between person and collective by amplification of individual movements with analogy to procedures used in the analysis of individual and collective rites. This is both a psychological method and an anthropological technique which takes into account institutional structures, cultural conditioning and implicational meanings comprehended by way of inter-related symbols, motivations and framing behaviours. In the majority of cases these, rather than proven factors, have informed our present-day knowledge of psychic behaviour and the work of depth analysis.

Unfortunately, not all 'happenings' which the uprooted youth of Western society encountered on their journeys honoured their naive motivations by providing or nurturing responsible understanding of the ritualized adventures they were ready to embark upon. Some, of course, have found satisfying and lasting solutions to life's dilemmas and when they have, the solutions have also revealed similar and identifiable characteristics. Psychologically, these people have been able to release, discover or restore a balance within themselves, a balance that is linked with acquiring a sense of subjective purpose and choice. Thereby they have been forced to confront their own ethical decisions and choice. This has not always been comfortable or rewarding since it has been notably in conflict with the ideas and ideals of the most staunch guardians of values against which youth initially rebelled. Their migrations have challenged loyalties to family, church, welfare and state.

Understandably, without seasoned guidance, some have misread and over-rated certain aspects of their experiences. They have been impetuous and at times have projected their own idealistic solutions onto alternatives with the zeal of converts. But some of what they have found 'works' for them and we who have sought or practised holism from the outset, certain pioneering doctors, philosophers, parents, priests, teachers, spiritual guides and in-depth psychologists, are now forced to revise our own methods. For the question remains as to why we could not meet the felt needs of these seekers in the first place.

Speaking collectively, from the time of their foundings, major religious and psychological schools have looked upon variation as deviance and schism, as a false and lamentable division of a single united and infallible truth. There are reasons for such a bias, reasons that have been well rehearsed and analysed.[9] If we adopt this perspective, however, we cannot help but see the advent of New Age therapies and present-day shifts in religious practices as fractious and threatening. Our reactions become passionate and inflamed. We oppose what we interpret as schismatic and divisive tendencies in alternative approaches and we either condemn or insistently try to reconcile them.

In the case of the churches attempts have been made to reunite diversity by way of an ecumenical vision. Politically and economically, efforts are made to accommodate, satisfy and incorporate diverse peoples in ever larger units. Sociologically, sub-groups such as Blacks, gay men and lesbians establish counter-cultures and outline politically correct attitudes expected in relation to those who deal with them. But in this instance the problem is not one of splinter or sectarianism. It is fundamentally archetypal;

that is, psychological and, being psychological, personal and religious as well as political and historical.

Caught as we are in the frustrations engendered by the irreversible break-up of cherished traditions and attendant power struggles set in motion since 1960, few of us have dared allow ourselves sufficient space for reflection in order to identify the underlying factors that would affect persons so strongly that they feel impelled to reject what was defined as a comfortable lifestyle on the assumption that there is an as yet undefined but alternative way of doing things. Therefore, threatened and dislodged from a myth of security, there has been a resurgence of fundamentalism and fanaticism throughout the Western world.[10] But what does one see psychologically in this instance if one approaches the situation that has confronted us from the perspective of depth and as if it were an extended case history? To do so involves an encounter with symbol and symbolic behaviours indicative of unconscious futurity as well as previous conditioning.

It is psychologically predictable that insistence upon unity constellates diversity. From the outset of depth psychology we have known that 'the forsaken "other" must inevitably appear; the repressed return'.[11] This other is indeed returning, emerging from the shadow, even as we have predicted and assumed that it would. But interpreters must take care that our attempts at understanding do not partake of the same shadow elements that encouraged and, indeed, insisted upon repression.

If we look around us at what is apparent and near at hand, evident from our own life experience and that of persons close to us, we discern an approach to change made evident in the search of New Age seekers from the outset, discern it from hints dropped like pebbles along the way as if to guide the footsteps of others to awareness of a morality relevant to the unease we feel about circumstances though incommunicable in words we have used heretofore. Yet, to discern these markers we too need to 'get with it' and take a path untried and unacceptable in terms of previous patterns of belief and loyalty. Symbolism reveals; we can no longer attempt to prove – or, worse, assuming we have already proven, to insist.

One of the first markers characteristic of the advent of the New Age was the disestablishment of values vested in the social institutions of family, education, church and state that represented traditional authority; i.e. a dis-ease with the status quo combined with a sense of ominous fear about the future. In terms of the persons who experienced that time, it began as protest and bore the hallmark of student protest. The first outbreak was at Kent State University in Ohio and then protest began to spread like a wave around the world while elders of the first generation who found themselves challenged countered with appeals to reason, putting their trust in common sense, law, order and the wisdom of an established ethic. The mistake was to assume that actions fuelled by such intense subjective emotions were amenable to objective reason.

Today, with hindsight, if a more conscious psychological perspective had been taken, those involved with oversight might have perceived that what was happening was an emotive outburst fostered and triggered by the power of long-withheld emotions and outrage. But in the heat of the moment that would have appeared to take too long and public consciousness was not ready for that. So, without willingness to acknowledge that signs pointed to protest triggered by a primal and archetypal impulse subjectively registered, it was met with frustration, anger and resistance. Like Oedipus, those responsible took the situation personally and, despairing at the loss of their innocence, blinded themselves.

Again, there have been many articles and well-documented reports written about the outbreak of protest, some of them by psychologists. But if we had been able to claim the psychological distance necessary for reflection, had we viewed the phenomenon as if it were part of a collective dream; that is, a phenomenon rooted in an unconscious complex, we might have adopted different attitudes. We would have discerned that it was fuelled by the power of long-repressed possibilities and hopes that had been projected onto those same governmental, educational and religious institutions that were being destroyed, all of which were dedicated to the perpetuation of established objective and patriarchal values. Furthermore, pursuing beliefs with such zealous fervour, might not both sides have sensed that the battle took on aspects of a crusade?

Supposing we had brought to analysis of these outer events the same awareness that one expects to apply in relation to happenings in the inner world, we would have noticed a recurring and tragic mythological motif; namely, the intransigence of an historic and educational power which reinforced beliefs and standard assumptions enthroned at the centre of our cultural consciousness. The public ego was one in which the logic of scientific reason and a faith in development had come to substitute for the *Logos* of revealed Truth. Collectively we had little flexibility. This was the time when all stories of relevance broke down. There was no recourse to a symbolic or mythic awareness from which we might have drawn insight and imagination. Contemporary attitudes had so played down the place for relative ritual accompaniment to conscious living that it had to be re-discovered in unconscious life.

Unfortunately, nothing in modern religious or psychological practice had adequately prepared us for the magnitude and manner of this protest. As a consequence the ones most passionately and painfully involved had to devise their own rituals of change. While in pursuit of a renewed myth of meaning, one can say those in search of initiation had to become their own initiators.

To speak of initiation now is to address a different consciousness from that of the 1960s. What signified the symbolic awareness of those days centred primarily upon two insistent messages, one being the need for journeying and the other for re-visioning in isolation and independence. What would then be enacted would be neither adaptive nor illustrative for it could not be based upon remembered rites. Nor was it an experiment. It sprang from a motivation to get beyond an old and familiar environment and to open oneself to the language of inner promptings. Such desires have characterized psychological preparation for initiatory experience from time immemorial. The sharp, stark cleavage of society's historic image which plummeted twentieth-century youth into liminality triggered a drive for action dependent upon both an urge to rid oneself of something along with an urge to incorporate something.

All initiations are fostered by a drastic change of conditions which produce dislocation, restlessness and disorientation in the individual. He or she then undergoes a process of reorientation that is total. Whether or not this is a prelude to more full and satisfactory living will depend upon the openness with which that initiatory process is conducted and registered. For initiation is the ritual which is introductory to a new state of being in which it is possible for someone to relate creatively to changes which have created new circumstances. One's sense of time, one's image of oneself, one's values, one's sense of who one is and what for are all transformed.

Facing the onslaught of change that began in the 1960s, the more daring of the youth involved turned instinctively to other forms that would again bring conscious and unconscious forces into a different balance within themselves. To do this they had to adopt the outsiderhood indicative and characteristic of liminal status. They dressed differently; they spoke differently; they devised new forms of communal living, all of which set them apart from the rest of society. Separation from parents, anonymity, solitude, hardship, poverty, the seeking of visions, exposure to risks and bonding with other initiates have all been part of *rites de passage* for those passing from one stage of life to another in earlier societies.

In the 1960s and 1970s the difference was that the rituals had to be self-initiated, self-chosen, by and large self-administered and for the most part self-interpreted. They were like self-envisioned dreams deprived of the supportive companionship and mature wisdom of elders upon whom the initiates could rely. Civilization at that time provided no such seasoned and recognized figures. Some found their gurus but this too happened more or less by chance for at the outset of their journeys relatively few dared venture beyond reach of modern telecommunications.

Nevertheless, a reciprocal and trusting connection was established or re-established with certain ritualized practices of mediation between near and far worlds, the world within and the changing world outside. This opened the way for the inclusion of ancient and ritual forms in New Age therapies, so called, and stimulated the recycling of religious practices, providing a different mythic and structural undergirding to belief and practice. But coinciding with the disestablishment and decline of Christian worship, extremism manifested itself in many forms as well, both blatant and subtle. Caught in the swirl of change, frightened and eager seekers asked for gods who were immediately manifest and effective. They hardly stopped long enough to absorb their experiences and integrate the psychic and sacred realities to which they had been exposed.

Unfortunately, again the majority of parental observers and conventional teachers found any suggestion of relationship between New Age protest and religion unthinkable. To them it looked, as indeed it became for a number of erstwhile journeyers, like 'opting out'. But like religious heretics who had come before them the protestants were rebelling against an outmoded and inadequate view of God, although unlike such prophets and founders, they were not yet ready to substitute new meanings of godliness. Still, this did not keep them from breaking away and their protest at its core was, as a religious philosopher has so wisely put it, a protest 'against God in the name of the God beyond God'.[12] They went in search of new structures, new metaphors, new patterns on which new selves and new connections to society could be built. Transformation was the initiation they sought. This was the destination of their unconscious pilgrimage.

Ego consciousness has an affinity for light, for heroism and salvation. With the protest and disestablishment of the 1960s and 1970s came a darkening of the light; the paradox and ambivalence of change were introduced into everyday living while this in turn introduced a new perception of shadow. The reactions and conclusions of New Age travellers affirmed this. They were less sure. They no longer saw what had been defined as right to be irrevocably right in all cases; similarly the good could no longer be relied upon as unquestionably good. Shades and half-lights of feeling and belief became visible and here there was a shift from the certainty of reasoned ego conclusions to soul as a point of referral.

There was a turning inward. With this shift subjectivity was recognized and the place of ritual was re-established. Initiation to soul-experience revealed a need of gods and the gods' need of us. In the 'real world' of outer events it was becoming increasingly clear that neither our natural, political nor technological environments could long sustain us. As the psychiatrist and existentialist Karl Jaspers had warned, we began to see that we well might be 'in the last age of historical person'.[13]

Such knowledge and speculation foster anxiety and a despairing sense of urgency. Time changes as dramatically as when Sir Gawain was assailed by the Green Knight. We now confront this figure and it demands, as ever, a transformation of attitudes pertaining to life, death and futurity. With that confrontation the frontier of conquest becomes the human soul.

The central experience of all initiands is an experience of dying to a world that was, including images of oneself, in order to expose the core of the person to come. Here a majority of those individuals who set off naively and untried later discovered themselves to be pilgrims on a subjective and sacred journey, pilgrims, that is, as defined by two long-term observers of pilgrimage process, the anthropologists Victor and Edith Turner:

> A pilgrim is one who divests himself or herself of the mundane concomitants of religion – which becomes entangled with its practice in a local situation – to confront in a special 'far milieu', the basic elements and structures of faith in their unshielded, virgin radiance.[14]

Distinctions between initiation and pilgrimage itself are subtle but later the effects become increasingly apparent. There is an initiatory quality in pilgrimage. There is a certain similarity in the trials undergone. Psychologically, they proceed along parallel lines but with the distinctive exception that at the climax of pilgrimage the pilgrim is exposed to consecrated objects and insights indicative or symbolic of sacred and secret or subjectively attuned teachings. The first wave of New Age seekers reinitiated us to the psychic reality of initiation itself which metaphorically and symbolically reopened pilgrimage routes within the soul as well.

'The innocence of the eye is the whole point here, "the cleansing of the doors of perception".'[15] For, ultimately, receipt of the secret gnosis, its effect, is individual and indescribable. It is a movement of the heart, a knowledge of the soul sacred to the receiver or enlightened one, a receipt of knowledge of the unknown God beyond God and it manifests as a change of being.

If asked, the majority of New Age seekers would not have admitted that they went in search of the unknown God and would have rejected the suggestion of their being *en route* to a sacred destination. Yet, facing the world's night and prepared by their disillusionment with modern society, they turned into the abyss of solitude on the track of fugitive gods. What was revealed was a way to renewed sacred experience and expression. The experiences themselves granted neither status nor wealth, but, given the travellers' motivations when setting out and the fact that the majority of them headed for the Far East, it is not surprising that today the fastest growing religion in the English-speaking world is Buddhism[16] – Buddhism which in any of its many forms is one of the most individually ritualized, subjectively received and inwardly focused of all religions. They returned to the West with a gift that was holy.

Psychologically speaking, pilgrimage is not a rite realizable in its happening. It is a way of pursuing Truth which may not become apparent until much later. The journey is an individual one involving hardship, risk and loneliness. Its measure consists in the way by which the sacred, formerly hidden and unimaginable, reveals itself as the measure against which one measures oneself. When the pilgrim returns to everyday existence one feels a new leaf has been turned over, that it's the beginning of a new chapter, he or she has made a spiritual step forward.

But for this to be lasting a record must be kept that outlives memory and to which one can turn as a journal of selfhood. The record may be kept by a group and evidenced in fraternal vows of some sort but there needs also to be the accessible and lasting account for the individual. Such records become personal scriptures whereby an account of my doings gives an account of myself and to myself. Whatever other reasons may be advanced, pilgrimage, after all, is a ritual journey undertaken in search of Self. The record records one's encounter with sacred and private Truth. Eventually it becomes a story in which I account for myself subjectively and morally.

At the end of the twentieth century society as a whole is gripped by a search for alternatives. Each of us is left alone with the option of creating our own style. Realization and integration are attempted but, despite frequent references to holism, parts are still shown preference over design or structure. Encounter is given precedence over long-term relationship. Our view of life becomes cinematic.

On the moving screen we discover a way to explore alternative selves while circumstances tape us for stereotypical and politically correct reactions. Culturally we are very close to the state exemplified by André in which the received command was simply to keep moving. Having disestablished social boundaries and dethroned previous gods, all that is retained in consciousness is an identity programmed by a running script that tells one to go on. By analogy, millions become cultural fugitives.

Until there is trust we can only flee; yet it is the nature of psyche to work upon events and their connection to a personal condition. To recognize our fugitive condition already is a shift away from submission to a running script towards personal awareness and the possibility of reflection upon the story unfolding. Significantly, this becomes a shift from object to subject. And I wonder if it is not here, in the shift from seeing ourselves as objects to viewing ourselves as subjects, a shift symbolized by the recovery of an ability to record and listen to the unfolding of individual stories, that we may discover hope as persons and as citizens in a world drastically in need of recycling.

Lifestorytelling began as a therapy on the fringes of society and at the last staging posts of life – with wanderers, with those who were alienated and exiled, persons who had suffered break-downs, with abused and tormented children, in Third World set-tings, with refugees, protestants and prisoners, among men and women who were victims of discrimination as well as with those afflicted by senility and approaching death. These were people for whom the script of the historic and collective story had lost its relevance and/or virtually come to an end. Lifestorytelling became central to the recovery of their voices and the trans-mission of values just as it had been central for the preservation of oral traditions in the past. Its resurgence in the form of journal-ling during the 1960s and 1970s was, once more, a revival of a 'soul memory' retained somewhere below the level of demands imposed by the prevailing ego consciousness of the collective.

One's lifestory replays life's epic for its reader. One can say that a vision incarnates itself in the work and completes its exist-ence therein for the vision functions in the psyche with reference to an image of the object that guides it.[17] The means chosen are in relation to the conditions of that vision. With awareness of this, life presents itself as both an artistic and an ethical venture, a production in which the vision that prompts and the results produced are seen and valued from both perspectives, that of an objective presence and I, the subject of my life.

It is an emotional connection with life's running script that turns it to story with the capacity to involve both teller and listener in the narrative. And this brings soul into history, reveal-ing the story in such a way as to make it possible to participate meaningfully in the street theatre of a generation for inevitably involvement brings the chief actor, oneself, to thresholds of dis-covery and choice. Freed from the notion that there is something or someone 'out there' who pulls the strings and sets the stan-dards for what I can or cannot, must or must not do or say; freed, that is, of ego submission to an idealized image of someone or something that exists prior to and independent of what I am and can make of my life's experience, I am also freed to use my imaginative powers to fantasize a role not merely as actor but as something of a co-author and dramatist as well. Hence, as my story unfolds I am involved in a process of devising my own myths and fables which the future chapters of my life inevitably tell onward.

I am not always conscious of the myths I live by, of course, nor the allegorical meaning of the fables I enact but the tales have the potential of being made conscious. And, by careful reading and re-reading my story from time to time I become aware of certain implications. Re-reading can be a form of reflective meditation and as perception deepens, I can consider revising my responses and reactions, admitting to myself that, given a change of attitude on my part at certain points, another mythologem might be given precedence and a different tale told. Or I suffer awareness that there have been moments of decisive change that, regretfully, someone, I, myself, let slip.

It is as if at such moments life attempts to rebalance itself, making use of psyche and its complexes to enable someone to participate in the creation of an individual story which in the final analysis can be seen to have been of worth. With honesty, such moments of arrest and challenge provide for a moral and ethical confrontation with meaning. These are the 'unique nuclear moments, the heroic moments through which the archetype at the soul's core is revealed which redeems events from the blindness of mere fact'.[18] The 'archetype at the soul's core' has been variously named by persons of different religions and psychologies as God, by Jung as Self or The Archetype of Transformation but universally recognized as the Sacred and that of Truth in every person.

Without a sense of personally recognized Truth we have no sense of history beyond a case history. We do not enter it; remain spectators or reporters rather than participants. Journalling then becomes journalistic, a record kept without concern for inward and central meanings. In contrast, Hillman reminds us, 'This core of soul that weaves events together into the meaningful patterns of tales and stories recounted by reminiscing creates history.'[19] The remembrance of things past reinforces a sense that there is more to someone's life than one finds in the facts alone. It is an experiencing of individuality related to relevance of some kind.

But this shift requires a change in what we allow ourselves to recall. It encourages us to string events together psychologically, ritually, with respect and reverence for my-self and the world-self rather than for an ego-self, victim of circumstance. It softens the polarities involved in decision-making and by introduction of feeling insists that I recognize the presence of conscience or need for moral choice. It cleanses and atones for my misuse of personal resources.

It is especially because of her dream that I now wish to introduce Amelia. Amelia had been a silent protestant through all her adult years although a woman forced by circumstance to stay close to home and the facts of her personal life. Nevertheless, time and again she noted a repeated and similar challenge presented to her at different stages and under different circumstances. Time and again also well-meaning professional consultants shook their heads, saying, 'I really don't think you have any other choice except to . . . I can't imagine how you can do anything else but . . .'.

So Amelia was nearly seventy and approaching death when, with the help of her own soul-directed reminiscence, she realized she could and in fact she felt she must do something else besides. . . . Though the situation had not outwardly changed, her attitude to the problem changed. She chose another course. This meant the sacrifice of a long-held ethical assumption rooted in the experience of early childhood and many times reinforced. Fortunately, since the essence of all sacrifice is a giving and a receiving, the sacrifice rewarded her with a consequent discharge of energy by way of which she was able to live her death rather than merely to die to life. But by the time that Amelia found sufficient courage to confront the irrational summons of her life she was an old woman and she had lived a stress-ridden and divided, albeit what was judged by others to be a selfless and 'God-fearing' life.

Her last reported dream was this:

'A box has been put unexpectedly into my hands. It is the size of a hat box but square. Inside there is a tape wound round and round a spool. A single line is imprinted upon the tape. I hold the box in my lap and read the story line imprinted on the tape again and again. I read it day by day or more often and I suddenly realize why the wise have been so from the beginning of time. It is by keeping in touch with this emerging story and following it – ticker-tape or fax or diary.

Some folks who are standing around this large post office room where I have received the box are surprised that it has been put into my hands. I am also amazed but I am not going to let anyone who may think me unworthy part me from it now that it has been given to me. It is very precious and private but I feel it belongs to me and enables me to be part of all time.'

The word conscience, *conscientia*, presupposes a schism within the self as a result of which our inner psychic life stands confronted by itself as with something foreign. 'My conscience tells me,' we say, as if conscience were a separate and superior voice; but it could say nothing of the sort if it were not already integral to myself. Thus, it must be something foreign to one's working identity, a kind of demon or daimon, that disrupts life either to torment or to fulfil it – perhaps both. To the story-telling self it cries out for subjective recognition saying, 'I *too* am part of the story you are telling. The story of your *I* is also the story of *me*.' Fortunately, Amelia heard its cry in time to release her radiant song.

Accompanied by disruption and denial the demon or daimon of change makes its appearance and by its insistence we discover that moral truth is not simply objective, 'out there' and waiting to be applied; it is subjective and inside, waiting to be acknowledged and used. This recognition embraces the dichotomy between ego identity and self image. What was felt to be a struggle between the two finally emerges as a story of two selves meeting. The self which desires simply to live and get on with it is compelled either to avoid or to summon resources to accept that other self as a kindred being.

The recognition of the inner and irrational voice of the soul either as foreign and harmful or as benign, perhaps even sacred, brings to the human person a certain firmness and resolve. Moreover, at this juncture one's own story becomes infused with the sacred by partaking of both worlds at once, the human and the divine. The most profound gratification for Amelia from her dream was that her story was acknowledged to be part of all stories and their wisdom. It was not the content of her ultimate choice that made it ethical; subjective choice in conjunction with the divine is itself ethical. What conveyed evidence of that to her was also evidence of 'all time'. Her time was 'all time' universal time, and her story happened 'once upon a time'. At that point, a life was freed to tell its full story onward, the seminal core of which was subjective and individual but an individual story with an ethical storyline becomes a parable.

By implication, from a psycho-religious perspective, this is a somewhat different story from the story someone recounts on the spur of the moment. The imagination from which it springs and the listener to whom it is addressed are felt to be one and the same, the subjective psyche. Using this as a starting-point, we can see that if we distort that story into an archetypal and heroic epic, we stamp on the throat of an incarnate song. It is not knowledge or obedience that enables us to sound our individual voices but disciplined, attentive befriending of the radical and ritual moments of decision when an irrational summons intercepts the onward linear drive of the rational ego. Story will have the possibility of becoming sacred at that juncture when the irrational and impenetrable poses the problem of alternatives. To this we have been reintroduced in a New Age.

At the end of *A Portrait of the Artist as a Young Man*, James Joyce has Stephen Dedalus write in his diary: 'Welcome, O life! I go to encounter for the millionth time the reality of experience and to forge in the smithy of my soul the uncreated conscience of my race.' Once conscripted into the plot of an individual story someone is able to interact with its narrative. And, to put it in religious terms, by way of the ensuing involvement more of God has a chance of becoming person.

Times of psychological conflict are times when ethic is discovered alongside a personal morality. What is new and wondrous here is that the 'particular', 'the merely human', 'the only once' become interesting, seem attractive and are determinative. Conscience or the awareness that moral choice is subjective and that, as Cupitt says, 'moral truth is out there waiting to be found and published' reverses the previous teaching that we derive our place and value in the narrative of the divine by mimesis and reiteration.[20]

A relationship to and direct confrontation with the extra-mundane point of reference codified in the creeds is recovered. So far as story is concerned, the ego does not invent morality but recognizes the need for it and integrates it. As the vision of an artist is the intermediate determinant between the subject and a world waiting to be, I assume the role of artist in regard to my own person.

At times of crisis the author is felt to be dominant and the narrator self-effacing. But both of these are 'I' persons. My 'self' is my own – not yours or anyone else's. We have to look instead at the origin of our text and where it is coming from. The voice of the transcendent that breaks through not in a flash of insight and revelation but in the shattering of the *I* poses certain questions: 'Where is my god coming from? What is his or her standpoint and how does he or she derive the authority to script my performance? Whose show is this anyway?' Then comes the astounding and humbling perception that, 'If my God is not a separate character in my story, he or she must be available and the same as I.'

We assume that the stories we tell are about ourselves but they are also stories of our gods. There is a sacred element in that which is brought out in the unfolding of the plot itself rather than in the style we make use of when expressing ourselves. Ritual is not to be entrusted to prescribed performance; it lives and is person. 'The form is like a baited trap to which the spiritual process responds spontaneously and against which it struggles.'[21]

It is possible to live a good life without noticing its style but it is impossible to live an ethical life without consciousness of the images with which one struggles and suffers. They too figure in a life story and their interventions are determinative. The Sacred is one of them. This is to say that life's story is compounded of more than life's events. It is bound together by a deeply unconscious web of significance. Caught in that web we wrestle not only with an either/or or a shall I/shan't I but with an *and* and *I must*. To discover ethic in the irrational one has to go very deep, however, something one seldom if ever does voluntarily. Merely remembering or releasing is never quite enough. One is satisfied only when one joins the meaning of one's history. These are moments of recognition that emerge or stand out from attentive listening when choice is acknowledged as a consequence of being lent life. One could say that the art of lifestorytelling is in our interweaving with the fundamental patterns in such a way that we discover that bit of God with which we are able and content to live.

There is more to the notion than that the disestablishment of the New Age has destroyed the bogie of realist ontology called God, the cherished institutions of the Enlightenment or the patriarchy. It has also prepared the way for a new exercise of the imagination, new and very old but directed at a different outcome. We are now able to see with greater clarity how we have collaborated and colluded with a story telling us.

New Age followers have been condemned as irresponsible and disruptive. We have blamed them for the break-up of a dependable morality. It is true that our custom of morality was destroyed with the advent of the New Age, the disestablishment of accustomed social habits and institutions, including those of the Church, and deconstruction of our thought. But by way of search, exposure to encounter, a growing consciousness of the interaction of inner and outer worlds, experimentation with new patterns of relationship, ritual conversions and observing the storylines of their lives, New Age people have also recovered a religious vitality from obsolescence.

In their demonstrations against codes of objective morality they have uncovered a subjective ethic in which the gradations between good and evil are no longer marked out as on a spectrum but take the form of a circle or spiral without linear polarities. They defy opposition but they discover limits and, when they reach those limits, they convert as if responding to the pull of an incoming tide to achieve ethical balance. Some lose their balance and are swept away as victims of epidemic inflations. But through refusal to honour what is to them a diseased and decadent interpretation of *Logos* they come again to celebrate life in partnership with the sacredness of a story trying to be told.

To discover the storyteller's art of living they have had to expose themselves and die to what they saw as a fiction and a lie. The only force they have had with which to resist is a spiritual force that lay neglected at the opposite end of the spectrum from the authority against which they first felt moved to protest. Through use of it they have wakened Western society to creative freedom by way of a subjectivity in search of itself. This they regard as the brightest and most precious talisman one can find in life and they have placed it as a marker along the journeyer's path to an uncertain future.

Chapter 6

Prisoner of a thousand faces

His revolt is an attempt to live within the truth.

Václav Havel

Those who are struggling with their life's story all suffer dislocation and alienation but not everyone has the strength to follow
through to the point of ethical confrontation and truth. The exile,
the fugitive and the political prisoner, of whom there are many
in today's world, almost always get stuck at a point beyond which
they cannot go with forgiveness. Yet, in the human psyche, as in
the splintered society, there resides a longing to belong. So while
circumstances become more and more chaotic and our ability to
influence them diminishes, we are attracted to that which will
grant us the power we lack. Inevitably such times are witness to
the resurgence of once-abandoned gods who rise in new forms.

Frustrated in a search for influence and authority, artificial
distinctions between spiritual, intellectual and bodily healing dissolve against the will to power and our human yearning for
release from anger, anxiety and guilt. The hope of a saviour
revives. We aspire to lay hold upon the miraculous force of
whatever gods we have known. In our day and age there are now
many who like the *logioi andres* of the Greek world in the sixth
to the fourth centuries BC wandered the face of the earth promising cure. This ancient 'man of words', we are told, was not exactly
a story-teller, not exactly a chronicler, not exactly a magician; he
was all these and something more also.[1]

By admission, Empedocles who was one of them and who
permitted himself to be crowned as a god and worshipped by the
people reported that thousands followed him to discover where
the road to salvation led. Some desired oracles; others enquired

about diverse diseases 'in order that they might hear some little word bringing relief for', as he said, 'they had been writhing in harrowing torture for a long time'. His descriptions suggest to us familiar scenes.

As we approach the twenty-first century AD our rituals evidence more and more dependency upon the exotic, the otherworldly and the irrational. Here is symbolized the intensity of a longing for release that is total. Re-enacting the psychological truth that what we are not yet and may become is found around us in projection somewhere, most of us fail to recognize or dare not face the possibility that the healer we seek is imprisoned in ourselves.

Yet the accused, the hostage and the prisoner are no longer strangers in our midst. We do not have to crowd the narrow streets of any city to watch the tumbrils pass. They take their tragic journeys before our very eyes; we cannot avoid them. At a time when our Western outlook upon the world was different we held to a belief in reason, justice, progress and salvation which to some extent shielded us from consciousness of the suffering and tragedy that are the prisoner's lot but today we live in circumstances such that the sight of the prisoner is commonplace. Prisoners of an environment that we ourselves have created, night and day on television screens and in newspapers we are confronted with the condemned, their families and their stories. At the same time, depletion of our several worlds emphasizes we are become prisoners of ourselves.

Yet we find the isolation of the condemned is an alienation almost too terrible to bear. The scenes we witness arouse in us an uneasy feel of estrangement yet at the same time we sense a kinship with the convicted. We've been there; the landscape of that loneliness is familiar to us. The face of the one on trial has features similar to our own. Responding as if to a deep archaic stimulus we have an impulse to mask our identity, to wash our hands of a relentless guilt ... and with those fantasies a compensatory gap widens between us and the rich reality of life. For imprisonment and exile have to do with being in the world and forever condemned to feel an outsider.

The reactions that are energized when we hear mention of the prisoner spring from the archetype of the ego or *I*, myself, that same ego which mediates for us between consciousness and unconsciousness, energized by two psychic principles imaged as

Prometheus, the forethought, and Epimetheus who symbolizes afterthought. Ego gives us identity. Ego acts; with it we create history. Once Jung defined neurosis as 'ego division' for ego is the champion of consciousness and choice is its prerogative. Without its intervention we can easily become what D.H. Lawrence referred to as 'a mechanism, an assembly of various sections'.[2] Ego is the guardian and translator of being.

The function of ego, then, is mediation. I picture it as standing guard always at a border between consciousness and unconsciousness, allowing or forbidding the passage of energies, emotions, fantasies, impressions, experience and knowledge one way or the other and thereby enabling the conversion of possibility to phenomenon – possibility being an unconscious image; phenomenon being what appears. But the ego mediates that which is strange, suspicious and unacceptable in both directions, from outer to inner as well as inner to outer. In its fullest sense, then, ego's work, like that of any mediator, becomes a means of reconciliation for two distinct and separate entities that are intrinsically related to one another but never merge. The essence of each remains distinct to itself but their co-existence within psyche produces the unique person.

How does ego operate in relation to this process? From whence does it take its orders? Ego is that which registers and acts in light of such consciousness as I can command. So ego is not just the doer but also informs the doer. Ultimately, the actor is *I*, myself, a person. Ego can be described as the eye of my *I*, the ability both to hypostasize and enact an *I*.

> It is not something, neither is it of any kind or degree; it is not mind, it is not soul; it is not mood, nor again does it remain still; it is neither in space nor in time; it is in itself, of one kind, or, rather, without kind, being before all kind, before movement, before stillness for all these things concern being, and make it many.[3]

We do not usually speak of the ego this way. Rightly, this is the way we refer to the self. But there is nothing of the personal self I may not become if I can release what is imprisoned in my soul. Ego is the faculty entrusted with that realization.

To associate ego, as we are apt to do, with the working personality that we confront in everyday life is limiting and sidesteps the importance of its discernment and mediation psychologically.

On the other hand, Jung suggested calling the total personality – which, though present, can never be fully realized – the self and therefore he saw ego subordinate to self as a part is to the whole. But the idea of subordination minimalizes the significance of ego once again. For though its role is that of mediation it is also able to exercise judgement and choice so as to mediate in an individual way specific to human and personal conditioning, time and circumstance.

The possibility of realizing the *principium individuationis* resides with the ego and personhood is its visible form. As with all archetypal behaviour we must not mistake the semblance for the image itself and the operative processes that underlie it. Yet, the semblance is the thing itself expressed insofar as an ego is able to comprehend and enact it. And just as the image and the totality of the self is not lessened by becoming person, personhood is humanized self. Once the self is revealed in this way, however, it is no longer to be referred to as 'the self' but bears a person's name, one's own.

From henceforth one's name is no longer a label; it is a new actuality signified by a word. In the act of naming the self is authenticated in essence and in person. Long before humanity acquired the concept of personality, perhaps even before there was awareness of differentiation between body and soul we were beings with names. Names exist prior to persons. Calling oneself by name assigns to self and ego a definite form and settled content and thereafter my person is by no means an abstraction in the sight of others or myself. The Christian ritual of baptism wisely acknowledges that the *dramatis personae* of being are two represented in a single soul embodied.

In consciousness the rite of naming is equivalent to celebrating the kinship of soul and body. By this gesture someone lays claim to a nature that is one but with dual aspects and powers. The Greek term *daimon* so often used in modern psychology and presumed to be synonymous with the principle of individuation is merely a mode of expressing a belief that a certain effect is produced by a transformative source often referred to as an otherworldly or higher power.[4] The name of someone gives consistency to the presence of that power in a human person. Thereafter it has worldly identity.

To allow this is the consummate challenge of consciousness and here we find the connection between our secret fascination with the image of the prisoner and an immediate impassioned reaction to anything that reminds us of the presence of that image. It touches an ontological guilt latent and repressed in us all. We know the many times we have refused to incarnate a fragment of the self or confess, like Caliban: 'This thing of darkness I acknowledge, mine.' But we do not think the ego; we are it and inasmuch as we become aware of that, this calls us to attention and to account, decision and choice. Ready to act upon the summons of our dreams as well as other unconscious promptings and urges, ego remains the custodian of all we can ever know of being and without its help the persons we may become remain imprisoned at the border.

That which imprisons psyche takes many forms. One of the symptoms of imprisonment is a relationship to a god-image emptied of significance, without appeal, its lifegiving force bereft of aesthetic, physical or emotional relevance. Nothing any longer seems to matter to me and I no longer seem to matter to it. The vital relationship between a person and that person's environment visibly alters in such a way that one becomes a spectator. The outer world appears as strange, remote and unreal as the inner world. Threatened, one takes recourse to power uninformed by a sense of personal relevance and meaning. The ego wanders aimlessly, driven by an unconscious guilt.

It seems that throughout the ages we have fumbled to identify the seed principle of being and to define its relationship with the *principium individuationis*. Various archaic religions arose as projections of its image and force, design and purpose. Sacramental rituals came into use to confirm and reassure us of our participation in godliness. In our time and as a psychologist Jung has spoken of the *Logos* or world-creating principle as the real *principium individuationis*, asserting it is co-inherent with being.[5] It is expressed in the human psyche as the archetype and generator of transformation.

The condition now ubiquitously spoken of as depression was often referred to as 'loss of soul' by Jung. For centuries before that religious communities had described it as *acedia* or 'separation from God'. Curiously doctors, psychiatrists and most members of religious communities have approached this negative state as if the flame of the soul could be rekindled by diligent labour and testing. I am not so sure.

To the psychologist there seems to be no other way but to

return to the sorting shed at the border station where the ego first transgressed its honest boundaries. Ritual is what takes place there; it is where one observes how, in the words of Saint Gregory of Nyssa: 'The mind like a mirror was turned about so that instead of reflecting God, it received into itself the image of formless and rejected matter.'[6]

The unyielding sense of guilt which causes repetitive suffering and stands in the way of our fulfilling ourselves as individuals is a tragic guilt, tragic because it is barren and its accumulation demands expiation. We may not be aware of how such guilt is enmeshed with ultimate values or how it came to establish its priority over the ego and in the personality but we never feel free of its bondage. Its tentacles cling to us by day and steal the dark treasures of the night. We are convinced there is no escape without payment of an impossibly high price, perhaps the price of life itself. We forfeit a cost daily through loss of energy and enthusiasm, sorrow and shame but accounts are never settled.

How often an analyst hears the words, 'If only I were strong enough to overcome my guilt . . .!' This puts the onus of blame on the operative ego once again. But is it merely a matter of strength, endurance or will? There is a deep and secret collusion associated with guilt. It may be exposed by our defences but it is an intimate and private matter, a condition which only we ourselves can alter. Jung writes:

Only a fool is interested in other people's guilt, since he cannot alter it. The wise man learns only from his own guilt. He will ask himself, "Who am I that all this should happen to me?" To find the answers to this fateful question he will look into his own heart.[7]

This forthright statement comes as something of a surprise from Jung. If we wish to find the answers to our guilt he does not give us a pep talk, an empirical or scientific reference. He recommends that we go to the source of our personal feelings; the heart will reveal our loving. Here is an affirmation that release from guilt can be effected only by acknowledgement of that which we love. It is not a matter of intellect, nor even of faith, but of heart. Without the grace of an overpowering redemptive love there is no freedom from the possibility of what seems to be fated. Until then imagination is trapped and captive; the ego lies gagged and bound. This is the timeless message too of *Fidelio*; love is faithful.

A force is activated here which is neglected in heroic, patriarchal or behavioural interpretations of personal psychology. I speak of the neverending psychic impulse to achieve unity of being. Here it is expressed as the urge for release of the prisoner, that an outsider and an outcast be allowed to return to its world and become one with it. The impulse can be identified as an instinct of the self to become itself, which is the same as what Jung identified as the instinct for totality.[8] The repressed and tortured ego yearns to be valued and validated by the other, not simply to be exonerated.

Its image is that of a supreme value which we love and for which we would give our all. However or wherever the image of the beloved may be projected and carried, as it was by Leonora in Beethoven's opera, the moment this is recognized is a moment of encounter between a person's identifying picture and the soul's authentic image (or I and Self) and its message is always one of salvation. So, at the high point of one's personal drama, at the centre of a personal enactment, one discovers an instrument of salvation. At first it may be only acknowledgement of a right to survive for which we struggle but finally and inevitably we find ourselves, through guilt, linked with the survival of God or our gods.

But before we go further, let us consider the impact and impress of a sequence of dreams. My analysand did not come to me for spiritual guidance. He was a therapist and he came to me for therapy. He was also a university teacher and a seasoned poet who had been born of a father trained for the law. His childhood home was in the rolling, rugged country of the Borders between England and Scotland where he had roamed and hunted in woods and copses. But he was not a stranger to the eloquent cathedrals and ruined abbeys of that landscape either. He had been twenty in the 1960s.

The first of the dreams was dreamed when the person was already well along in analysis:

'I have to approach an Abbot, a Father of a monastery or someone similar, to ask for *wayleave* to run a watercourse across his ground. We are outside. He stands above me on stone jutting out from the wall, like a statue in a niche. I have with me a companion upon whom he vomits. Though I myself stand aside and avoid the drenching, it seems like ritual humiliation. The figure asks me if I am afraid of his power. I answer, "No." I look him straight in the eye, saying, "Don't mess me around. Just make a decision, *yes* or *no*." He nods and says, "Yes".'

Exploring this dream the analysand and I both felt a lowering in ourselves as if we were moving deeper into memories of the past, our own bodies and psyches. This was not an ordinary dream. It came without warning but produced neither bravado nor elation. We began at the obvious and conscious level with questions about vocation and associations with the figures of the Abbot, the dreamer's gut reaction to the humiliation of his unknown companion and suppositions as to the role of that figure. But analysis could not end there. We both sensed there was 'unfinished business' to be dealt with between the dreamer and the Father of the monastery, 'unfinished business' that involved anger, resentment, defence and dread.

The analysand knew and I also knew the place of the Abbot in the medieval monasteries of his Borders home where the Abbot was regarded as the Father of a monastic family with far-reaching powers over the government and worship of his house, its lands and its inhabitants, a man with the insignia of a Bishop and authority for the Sacraments and the spiritual well-being of his professed monks. Neither of us was going to be the first to speak. We fell silent.

The dreamer sighed and finally addressed me, saying, 'You know, I think I, we are neglecting something here. If it is true, as you psychologists say, that the dream isn't just any play but *my* play and I'm not just one of the characters but *all* the characters, then somewhere I must be the Abbot too.' There was a pause followed by, 'I guess that's what I've been avoiding but at least the dream confronts me with it.' There was a longer pause and then, 'Well, that's something of a shock but I guess I've always known it.'

Claiming *wayleave* absorbed most of our analytic hours for many, many weeks after that and at times the mystery and surprise of the negotiations could tempt us to forget this was a spiritual quest. To discover how to express the sacred by way of the human is surely the most difficult and amazing problem with which psychology has to deal. It is dread, not fear, that creates our reigning gods, thereby generating the tensions surrounding relationships between rational power, however that is labelled, and person. For the adapted ego wants to conform, whether this means a hastening away from or towards the 'Father', and shadow helps it to survive by suppressing the demand of something which appears unpleasant and more often like a demon rather than a daimon within. Likewise, the internalized judge all too readily denies and in the instance seems seldom if ever ready to affirm what I am meant to be. And this was so in this circumstance.

Release of the prisoner is realized at a given moment but integration of freedom takes longer. Time and patience are required before a healing process can occur and be assimilated. Both conscious and unconscious aspects of a person must be addressed and a loving relationship fostered to that which I was not and discover that I now am. 'Reflections of the heart' are involved and the reasoning of the heart asks for compassionate empathy and companionship. The ordering principle of an identity that had once formed and now re-forms must be accorded respect, be confirmed and celebrated.

Access to that ordering principle entails and has as its precondition surprise and, as witnessed by the existing ego, crisis as well as humiliation. We can expect that shock will bring in its aftermath a sense of betrayal and that crisis will beget dread and fear but it also begets reverence, the humble human attitude that enables us to enter into communion with a reality outside our own narrow limitations.

To reverence is to stand in awe of that reality, an implicate order beyond my ken but of which I discover I am a part and towards which I now recognize that I feel a responsibility. Disregard of that awe was called hybris by the ancient Greeks. 'In dread we may be blessed or we may realize we are damned but in the easy-going calm of someone who has altogether forgotten astonishment and amazement there is neither blessedness nor damnation.'[9] By way of passionate crisis, therefore, we are led to the pathic ground of reverent acceptance and hence to the self.[10] The ground across which *wayleave* was requested by the dreamer is the ground of that primordial image. Consciousness of the sacred character of the precinct, once it has been claimed, will always be retained. Psychologically, its location is in the borderlands of two wills, one registered as human, the other divine.

Each analytic session is an act played out in the here and now, arising from organisms inherently obedient to an implicate order. And the 'enfolded order' observable in each part contains the whole.[11] The analogy is the hologram. We have learned to use these words since Jung but I equate the web of implicate order with what he intended by use of the term 'objective psyche'. For, when we realize that the reality that is the configuration of the analytic hour is instantaneous, not illustrative of life but, like theatre, linked to life by analogy, we sense that analysis is a method which transcends discursive reason and scientific psychology. Like the ritual of church and theatre, it addresses images that touch people in memorable and life-altering ways.

'Travelling somewhere in the heart of the country,' the second dream began. There had been others, of course, dreamed over the course of a year or more but none which suggested the impact and resonance of this. Both my analysand and myself were convinced that even though it was separated from the first by such a long distance in time and experience, it nevertheless was connected with the dream of the Abbot. For one thing the texture and look of the stone suggested it.

'. . . I see what at first appears to be a statue or statues by the road but they become animated and begin to move. They appear to be made of grey stone and would be gritty to touch if I were close enough. I watch from a distance and realize one of the figures is a man-type of creature and the other is a tree and they are dancing. I wonder if the creature is mythological but as *he* turns in a particular profile to me I recognize the appendages are wings and he is an angel. I am truly excited and know from somewhere that he has a name and this suggests there could be others.

The scene shifts to a bar or café where I sit in company but beside a man who is handsome, curly haired and naked from the waist up. I place my hand on his back between his shoulders and realize I am searching for where his wings were or are attached. He looks at me and says in a kind of conspiratorial way, "You can't go around showing who you are all the time." *We* know that *we* know he is an angel.'

If I had not known the dreamer as well, if I had not trusted his psychological strength, or if we had not worked at such depth during the intervening months, I might have been tempted to see the dream as an extraordinary attempt at compensation. Instead, I saw it as evidence of an extraordinary daring to transmute distance from the holy into the deep joy of nearness. It had a striking quality of being 'just so' and not in any way did it give evidence of heightened ecstasy. 'A dream of a lifetime, I guess, and incredibly beautiful with a knowledge that it will last,' the dreamer said.

I report the dream here because it introduces a figure of significance not only to the dreamer but in this day and age of ritual abandonment. The image is that of 'an invisible companion', not too unlike the invisible beings to whom men and women turned increasingly in Late Antiquity and the early Middle Ages and whom they invested with the precise and palpable features of beloved and powerful figures personified in their own souls.[12] Such companions included the saints and, as here, the guardian angel.

Without befriending and protection by such personages the uncreated breadth of freedom to which one is exposed by the self can be overpowering and become a wasteland of potential. Freedom presupposes choice and creativity depends upon discernment as well as possibility. Otherwise there is only licence and confusion. One is tempted to overstep human and humane limits.

At the apex of consciousness men and women of Late Antiquity placed the invisible intermediary as protector.

Whether the protector was presented as the personal daimon, the genius or the guardian angel its function was the same; it was entrusted with the care of the individual in a manner so intimate that it was not only the constant companion of the individual; it was almost an upward extension of the individual. . . . The abiding identity of the self was in its keeping.[13]

One saw the image and recognized himself in him or her, a bringer of companionship and salvation.

Whether in times of crisis or in the day-to-day search for protection and inspiration, ego sensibilities were moulded by a relationship to such companions. I have no doubt that Philemon was such a figure for Jung and from the perspective of our need for understanding psychic imagery in religious terms I feel it is too bad that his work on the mana personality was not further extended. But the wonder of the appearance of such a personage in the dream of a late twentieth-century man is not that he comes but what he signifies. For that which in the phenomenon is significance and in psychology is perceived and spoken of as meaning is revealed to us personally by the heart, and his message of salvation is the offer of companionship. In aloneness the ego can envisage the face of a fellow human being rather than trying to visualize the shimmering presence of a bodyless power. To him we belong; he has chosen us.

Here I quote not from Jung but from William Willeford writing in *Feeling, Imagination, and the Self*:

> Reflections on the 'reasoning of the heart' have an important bearing on individuation. Jung meant this term to name a process of differentiation and integration by which one's personal identity is kept responsive to the self in such a way that that identity is drawn beyond the one-sidedness of one's present conscious outlook, of one's upbringing and of collective values unreflectingly assumed. This process may be said to have a logic, but its logic is emergent. . . . Though enduring attitudes, sentiments, and beliefs are necessary, they are vital only in process. In process the ordering principle of the self that has formed and that re-forms and revitalizes them is felt.[14]

The guardian angel is a companion of the way in a guise that the only-human cannot simulate. Whenever that function is personally projected, there is bound to be disappointment. If it is transferred, eventually it must be withdrawn. The dream figure satisfies something which is lacking in the only-human even as it is in the non-human figures of gods, daimons and constructs. It trembles on the frontier of ego and self as an eternal guarantor of witness, forgiveness and identity.

Behind the need to find the recognizable face of an intercessor we can sense the pressure of anxiety and a hope of amnesty. To ask forgiveness is to ask that what we have done and for which we feel guilty be seen *sub specie aeternitatis*, in the light of eternity. A desire for forgiveness is at the same time an acknowledgement of the extra-mundane community of which one is a member, against which one has sinned and one's covenant with it. Consciousness alone is not sufficient to bring about redemption. There is none until one can imagine that one can reach across the deep crevasse of uncertainty with a known human gesture of acceptance. As Kierkegaard understood: 'The antithesis of sin is not virtue but faith.'[15]

This calls for a reinterpretation of rites of initiation as perceived by psychology. Here myth celebrates reality by taking the event and setting it upon its own basis. Whether or not someone is sufficiently cognizant of it to acknowledge the change, after an initiatory event life transforms itself. One then conducts life religiously rather than because of religion. This is not the experience of the sacred as 'a sharp feathered word' but conveys the image of a passionate and tragic soul struggling to realize and celebrate the bound as freed.

Thereafter, reverence accompanies human action. This idea seems strange and unacceptable to anyone who has had a hostile and negative introduction to religion by way of dogmatic instruction. It is a very different experience, indeed, and can hardly be described in usual terms. In a curious way, living the present moment, whatever its pain, at once places it in a context, a context pervaded by a sense of intense meaning we find it hard to let go of. Henceforward life presents itself as an urgent message in need of reply; it seeks our participation. Nor does the finality remove us from the world but returns us to it more wisely and invested with dignity. When the imprisoned truth breaks forth, I see the face of my God and recognize therein certain features of myself.

Something that is tempting but in my view unwise is to regard the receipt of a dream or initiatory experience, however numinous or rewarding it may be, as the apex and culmination of one's personal revelation of the sacred. In the dream of the guardian angel the intermediary who once appeared so elevated, unapproachable and austere has come down off his pedestal and is to be recognized as companionable to ordinary life. So ordinary and companionable does he become as to bear a resemblance to someone one might meet even in a café and, surprisingly to a dreamer, 'much the same as I'.

Because of personal circumstances there had to be a lengthy interruption in my work with the dreamer of the two dreams. Months passed without our seeing one another but when he returned he brought with him a recent dream that spoke again and directly about the tone of the relationship between the sacred and himself. He had dreamed it just after the purchase of

a new pair of walking boots which he was wearing. He hadn't
had time to record it yet, he said, but spoke it from memory.

'I was holding one of my old walking boots in my hand; it was
the one I would have worn on my left foot. The boot had split
and I was inspecting the sole. The inside of it was stuffed with
some sort of honeycombed material and impregnated with a
substance that smelled like methylated spirits.

Poking my finger around in the honeycomb I found a thin
strip of metal. What type of metal it was I don't know but I
was able to dislodge it and get it out so that I could look at it.
It seemed as if it were foreign to the shoe, maybe a missing
part of something else but, then, how did it get in there? It
was a curious little object. Whatever it was for, it could be
bent or maybe the two ends could be clasped together to make
a ring.'

The dreamer now smiled wryly. 'When I woke up the dream
puzzled me,' he said. 'I couldn't make head nor tail of it. I just
couldn't see what it was about and then suddenly it dawned on
me, "My God, it's about soul and spirit, of course!" '

To observe and interpret archetypes as the experience of primarily sacred forces enables us to consider our unfolding story
with consciousness of a fundamental power to help shape and
pattern existence. The self is then accepted as a fact of life. In
the moment I found I could not but answer, '*Your* God, *your*
soul, *your* spirit' – and I smiled too.

In attempting to write this I become aware of how limited the
language of depth psychology is. It lacks exactitude precisely
because the phenomena it seeks to describe are not repeatable.
No two neuroses are ever the same; similarly, no two revelations.
The psychological experience is highly subjective and being subjective, unique. Therefore, life-altering events cannot be
explained; they can only be described. They cannot be replicated;
they can only be accepted as if destined to happen naturally at
the behest of a power stronger and other than that of the ego so
that an exchange takes place assumed to be of worth to both.

A ritual undertaking such as initiation is a stage set for that
exchange. It fails, however, when its outcome is overbalanced by
consciousness or if too great a freedom is allowed to the archetypal and unconscious forces at work or too little befriending is
shown for the insights that occur in the aftermath of the experi-

ence. Here religion, not psychology, mediates, religion being thought of as respectful observation given to the transaction taking place between the known and the unknown. To respect is 'to see with new eyes', to re-perceive.

Prisoners of our own guilt, we live with fear and dread in order to avoid risking such a confrontation with faith. Those plagued by conflict of interest are confined to repetition of the process itself and any promise of salvation or transformation remains unfulfilled. Jungian psychology has made much of the images of the hero and the divine child as prompters of initiation, again emphasizing the duality of ego and self. To accept the image which initiates initiation as that of the prisoner, however, describes it more accurately as it is registered psychologically. One responds to the cry of an unreleased person imprisoned without trial by the tribunal of an existent ego, a function which arbitrates and judges in obedience to an image of identity that is now outworn and irrelevant. Mythologically, as we know, all initiations are concerned with death and rebirth in some form. This is about the death of an aspect of my previous god-image and its rebirth as *I*.

It is impossible, I am sure, to regard such a process as capable of being charted in stages that can be consciously worked through in pursuit of a goal. That leads to further evaluation, so-called failure and an immediate increase of internalized guilt. The summons to intitiation is registered at some point as a personal and psychic life threat and at that time, when the transforming ego is most vulnerable, it instinctively asks for ritual containment.

What then happens does not yield to rational definition. A ritual enactment inevitably takes place in that space and at that time, an encounter between human and supposed divine forces, an exchange that results in a changed human identity and internalization of a renewed Word. The form of the enactment is not the principal factor but its power. The sacred is not decreased thereby but humanity is enhanced.

Initiation ritual celebrates process in its relationship to an original unity associated with a sense of oneness. It acknowledges ego release, affirms a new totality and invites an updated relationship to the greater Self. The personal dream reflects a symbolic picture of the whole, offering involvement to the extent a person can comprehend, imagine and risk involvement. This, I would imagine, was an invitation inherent in the dream of the left boot.

Likewise, the ritual engages us in a transitional but collective process symbolic of working through the demands of the implicate order referred to by Jung as the objective psyche. Thereby personhood is affirmed and acknowledged. Someone's self is expressed and revealed so that now, informed by ego experience and however socially adapted, it can never be mistaken for another.

The intense, reverent, though unconscious inclination towards oneness discloses a desire for reparation which leads to communion. The gap between the appearance of such a yearning in ourselves and its fulfilment is a space asking to be inhabited by remembrance, sufferance and anticipation. A *kairos* or 'penetrable opening' appears in the tightly woven fabric of psychic conduct. Before the next note sounds, taking up the theme of individuation, there is a pause.

A dancer writes,

> Where you are when you don't know where you are is one of the most precious spots offered by improvization. It is a place from which more directions are possible than anywhere else. I call this place the Gap. [Movement from here] is *original* because its origin is the current moment and because it comes from outside our usual frame of reference.[16]

It is alienation from the existential gap that induces the fugitive state; rejection of or non-admission of the longing for unity makes us refugees, psychologically. It is as if we carry identity cards stamped with names we cannot duplicate. So we content ourselves by signing with a cross, thereby condemning something of ourselves to seclusion and imprisonment. Perhaps we think that we do this consciously and with the best of intentions. But however deeply buried, in startling and illumined moments we sense an urge and feel the agony. An unacknowledged part of the soul cries, 'Out!'

It is a moment of creative decision without which the *I* concealed will dissolve or be annihilated. Life is ready for participation in an unlearned sequence preparatory for release, celebration and communion. Freedom can no longer be thought of as an illusion. An image of it exists and indwells; its tradition has become interior. An idealized vision of ourselves perfected is fatuous but can haunt and destroy us while the self that is ready to be what it is and become what it is becoming waits.

We long for a gift of grace without allowing for the responsibility we feel towards this 'other' image of ourselves to be
expressed. What affects us asks only for protective companionship. The gentle and reverse side of virtuous obligation is love.
We hear a voice from beyond the wall and we reply.

Chapter 7

If ritual dies

A holy theatre not only presents the invisible but also
offers conditions that make the perception possible.

Peter Brook

Something waits to be said. Thus far I have hardly spoken of
ritual in its collective aspect. Yet it is to the collectivity that
persons most frequently refer as crucial in determining their attitudes to ritual enactment and it is social institutions rather than
themselves that they regard as guardians of ritual power; i.e. the
Church, the state and the family. Even though we experience
ritual individually, it is discussed as a group phenomenon and
some of our most emotive reactions in response to ritual observance are expressed as if it were consciously designed and
demanded of us in conformity to a known source. Confusing the
inherent power of the enactment with the explicit power of a
group, we expose our projections as well as avoid recognition
of the generative, unchanging yet variable source which is the
foundation of all rite.

Ritual is a form, like a poem, that contains a vision within an
image and rituals derive their strength from an origin which is a
god-reverie or god-image, an originality that springs from an
extramundane or extrapersonal source. Nor does it seem sufficient
to speak of that source merely as archetypal which is another
way of saying it is strong, recurring, eternal and capable of taking
many forms. Its origin is an energy beyond human control, an
energy that originates form as well as defies explanation for the
rite is also a creation that, though emanating from outside, paral-
lels one's inner and unique condition. Occurring at the confluence
of two impulses, one impressive and the other expressive, it is
empowered by the depth of mystery which the receiver can per-

ceive and dares expose as being part of his or her own soul's image. So, even if orchestrated by collective consciousness, the vitality of ritual remains, nevertheless, in the keeping of each one of us and dependent upon the honest rigour of our individual soul work.

In keeping with good psychotherapeutic tradition, in this book I have emphasized the role of the ritual participant. It has not been mine to speak of the intent of the initiator of ritual practice nor its institutional guardians. Yet, I surmise that there is much to be learned from further investigations of social conditioning as well as acausal phenomena such as the synchronicities of crisis, shock, summons, visions and voices of command whether they appear in dreams or otherwise. The latter, however, are manifestations not of collective consciousness but of the collective unconscious, the place where psychology and religion, past and future meet. For ritual happens at a meeting point of worlds, the sacred or unconscious and the secular or conscious. To understand it we must explore nothing less than the dynamics of that confrontation and its contribution to communication and transformation of a totality both individual and collective.

Since psychology and religion intersect in ritual it follows that without regard for the presence of one or the other, ritual will die. It is constructed of the mutual interdependency of the two. It is a crossroads at which the differing imaginative models that we bring to the understanding of life changes converge. The symbol is the cross.

To cross is to signify. Those who cannot write their own names are asked to sign with a cross; it is the primordial signature.[1] Crossings are of significance, numinous, moving and unpredictable. It was Hermes, Messenger of the Gods, who was acknowledged as guardian of the crossroads in ancient Greece. There, where one is challenged by change of direction and choice, one encounters one's god and signifies both as oneself and to oneself as well as in relation to that other. Both the student of religion and the psychologist agree that: 'Rituals reveal values at their deepest level and [humans] express in ritual what moves them most', whether the rites are collective and sanctioned by society or individual.[2] Significantly, in the Christian tradition the first of life's sanctified rituals is that of being named. There one's human existence is affirmed and acknowledged in the presence of another recognized as God.

Since both psychology and religion are expressed at a time of ritual enactment, there is more than one way to envision such crossings, however. As a psychologist I often hear people speak of their need to reach the centre and the spiritual journey is often described as a journey to the centre. The mandala is accepted as a universal symbol of the centre and as expressing the totality of the centre. However, if imaged from the perspective of the sacred, in a sunburst of radiating energies the lines do not appear to intersect because they begin at the circumference. They are radii which erupt from the centre itself.

What is the experience of ritual, after all? Is it not the act of entering into the presence of the Holy? As Professor Hussey once wrote of an early Christian coming into a Byzantine church: when he or she entered the narthex or stood in the nave, the participant did not simply learn something about the great truths of Christian teaching but could also realize that as a person, he or she was present in both seen and unseen worlds at once.[3] So far as ritual is concerned, this obtains whether or not the rites are Christian and, at times, even whether or not they are consciously religious.

Ritual does not simply involve habitual actions; it includes routine but it is not routine. It does not only provide exquisite displays seductive to mind and spirit. It is a container that fulfils the needs of the unconscious as well as the conscious self and within circumscribed space provides for a reciprocal exchange between the two, spirit and body.[4] Ceremonies become ritualistic when equal value is granted to the place of man or woman and gods or goddesses alike. Within its defined and consecrated space the formed confronts the unformed and an individual is impelled to move towards the yet-to-be formed inside himself or herself. It works psychologically because it relieves, releases and carries the attendant psychic tension during periods of transformation.

Ritual *per se* does not ensure a safe passage from one state of being to another but it does ensure that the passage is marked. Initially it can provide sanctuary from a fate that is overwhelming and appears to be inevitable at that time. Later, one emerges with a sense of having been altered by exposure to an imagery of cosmic proportion yet by way of a metaphor that is personally relevant. Most importantly, it does not have to be contrived; it happens naturally.

Over the entrance of Jung's home there was inscribed a pre-

Christian saying ascribed to the oracle at Delphi and given in answer to the Lacedaemonians before they faced battle with the Athenians. The saying was: 'Invited or not, the god will be present.' It was an apt inscription for the threshold of a house belonging to one who would live a symbolic life on the border between conscious and unconscious perception, a life involving repeated encounters with his own god-image and that of others. The words are both chastening and reassuring for they suggest that the vitality of the god's presence endures however hard someone tries to avoid it or as difficult as it may be to discern. It is a reminder that human struggles will reveal the interface and interconnection between god-design and human-design.

The recurring questions forced to the surface by periods of trial are: 'Does it have any meaning at all?' and 'How can a god allow it?' That which happens at the centre reveals both answers. Ritual events are impressive because there we experience the *other* directly. This accounts for the rigid structure and formality of the rite. It exists in liminal space between worship and abandon, being and making. It must be sufficiently strong to withstand the force of that which is numinous and become the crucible for personal transformation. 'Problems can be solved; mysteries can only be lived.'[5] The function of ritual is to protect, enable and realize mystery.

When someone emerges from a ritual happening sufficiently to recover his or her bearings and a modicum of balance, he or she can know better the proportions of both the god-image and one's self, or, better still, the dimension of one's god as one's self. For the power with which one has wrestled conveys more than a sense of physical power; there is also communicated a sense of verification and confirmation of who one is and what one is about. Ritual process is soul-shattering. While it is happening, the defensive husk and shell of the personality are broken and the ego impregnated with awareness of something of its sacred nature. Consciously or not the image of a previous person lets go in communication with a stronger and more relevant summons. Personhood and its meaning are altered.

Unless, on the other hand, someone feels he or she can ignore ritual or disclaims it, avowing, 'It doesn't move me.' If this is the case, he or she is endangered quite as much as someone who may be caught up in identification with the numinosity of what is happening. In living ritual there is an interchange and for that to happen a relationship must be established between two separate types of being who seek and respond to one another. If the two never meet or when perchance they become one, individuality will die by exclusion. The one who purposefully excludes himself or herself can only be an outsider, present as an observer, perhaps, but not a participant in what takes place. And there is a loss to the personality as a consequence.

Until 1947 members of the caste of Untouchables were without identity in the cultural consciousness of India. It was Gandhi who first spoke of these people as Harijans or Children of God. Only then did the long, slow climb to personhood begin for them. Before that, they were automatically excluded from all forms of ritual participation. They had been accorded a status, it is true, for they symbolized the unclean, but as a group they were never allowed to enter the temple. They remained outsiders and by that exclusion they were deprived of opportunities for self-definition through conscious participation in living ritual. As a corollary, they were also deprived of a sense of self-worth.

Withholding or being withheld through acceptance of a projected or introjected status of oneself as untouchable, an individual suffers no encounter and registers no change of person when face to face with his or her gods, is not blessed by the interchange. Deprived of communion with that which one reverences but is not, one dies to significance. One's being is never affirmed by meaning and, like the Harijan, one must seek it alone and elsewhere. But what is more likely to happen is repression of the ritual impulse and a stultifying of the personality. For the burden of personal ritual definition is hazardous and difficult to enact in solitude, requiring the utmost courage and discipline.

The god-image serves individuation not by prescribing how someone should look or behave; that is, properly, in totality, according to an established ethical code or otherwise, but by engagement. It is the archetypal vitality of the restive god-image that calls us to an encounter which can enhance life by transformation of our belief to knowing and our knowledge to signification. But for this to happen, there must be an openness to receipt of the summons for engagement and a willingness to respond. Without that, neither the needs of the gods nor those of human souls are served.

I have wanted to stress the mutuality that is inherent in living ritual. Observances which are more than habituated performances of traditional ceremonies depend upon recognition of a duality and reverence for the unending mystery associated with sacred presence. Significance dies by exclusion of either the person or that person's recognition of the place of his or her god within, whether the exclusion be conscious or unconscious, witting or unwitting. But the encounter with the living God is not a commonplace event easily described. Wherever and whenever it occurs, and by whatever name the god is called – Yahweh, Allah, Shiva, Christ, Buddha or simply The Way, it evokes an imagery surprisingly startling and requires a language majestically humble.

At a time of ritual revision, such as that in which we live, we must safeguard such eloquence. As the worker with dreams or the serious writer of a journal is made aware, the rich wonder of a revelation can be lost in the telling; it is not to be tampered with. The question is not whether dream or rite can be explained but how it moves us. And we need wonder, as with texts, whether of poetry or scripture, what resources are lost in translation.

Yet paradoxically here where we are most at risk, we are also most helpless. For we cannot manufacture rituals; we can only respond to a felt need for them or the awareness that they are happening. They are not compounded of logic; they are inspired, set apart from mundane existence and invested with an importance that transcends their strictly physical limitations. For example, I can plan to make a pilgrimage, which is a rite projected in space, but I cannot possibly foresee what the pilgrimage will make of me. That depends upon the impress of the journey and the value I give to that mark of the presence of the sacred upon my life's experience.

Jung wrote:

A *value* is a possibility for the display of energy ... Energy in itself is neither good nor bad, neither useful nor harmful, but neutral, since everything depends on the form into which energy passes. Form gives energy its quality. On the other hand form, mere form without energy is equally neutral. For the creation of a real value, therefore, both energy and valuable form are needed.[6]

Here the psychologist leaves us uncomfortably bereft of a guide to value; he merely underscores its importance and its need for expression in form. Perhaps it is not surprising that these lines were included in a discussion of sublimation or that exercise of sweeping under the carpet, burying beneath the threshold of consciousness those things we don't want to face and covering them over with what he called 'a surface heroism and an infantile defiance of fate'. This we do with will and determination, as if we could retain conscious control of the course of our lives. But, later, he adds the assertion and warning that 'there is no *human* foresight or wisdom that can prescribe direction to our life, excepting for small stretches of the way'. Eventually we are brought face to face with 'an unknowable essence that we cannot grasp as such since by definition it transcends our powers of comprehension'.[7] This is where ritual mediation serves – therapy, spiritual guidance, meditation, the Sacraments.

But here a note of caution. Present-day short-term therapies frequently offer simulated ritual enactments as part of a package but the emphases seem to be on evocation of a mood conducive to exposure of repressed psychological memories and those who sign up for these workshops come expecting a 'happening' of dramatic and healing consequence, something like a do-it-yourself cure. Sometimes such expectations are fulfilled but relatively seldom is there adequate preparation for containment and nurture of what is revealed. Attention is focused on ego-adjustment instead. Ways of intervening or techniques for integration are used. The contemplation and wonder essential to sacred adventure are bypassed.

Revelation is never general; it is always special and received by oneself alone while its impact is total. Innovators and directors of workshop programmes need to be prepared to work with totality, bearing in mind that both aspects of the priest and the role of the therapist will be demanded of them. Most likely the processes awakened will need to be addressed over time, one-to-one as well as in groups and with awareness of psycho-sacred orientations. Otherwise, what has occurred may well be registered personally as a betrayal. Still, relatively few of the persons who advertise such encounters submit to long-term psychotherapy or spiritual guidance themselves and remain unaware of the psychological risks involved in what they do.

Yet ritual and enactment are closely linked and here I turn respectfully to Peter Brook who says:

A Happening can be anywhere, anytime, of any duration: nothing is required, nothing is taboo. A Happening may be spontaneous, it may be formal, it may be anarchistic, it can generate intoxicating energy. Behind the Happening is the shout 'Wake up!'[8]

But it does not say to *what*. To discern that there has to be dedicated follow-through of more than the emotions roused by the Happening, to implications for life and a lifetime context as well. The question of what we are searching for is raised again.

All those who attempt to practise psychotherapy in depth and as an art warn us, as did Jung, that we can anticipate the inevitability of recurring confrontations between known and unknown. We can be prepared for uncertainties. We are to expect that periodically we will reach the limit of our ego resources, determination and insight and that we will suffer times of doubt when we will feel impelled to seek afresh knowledge of who we are in order to realign ourselves with as-yet-to-be-disclosed purposes. In such statements there is recognition of a need for mutual dialogue between seen and unseen forces, conscious and unconscious, sacred and secular patterns that will require ritual referral and clarification lifelong.

The question is frequently posed as to what Jung himself 'believed' or 'knew' in relation to sacred energies and divine purposes and it is often posed in the hope that what he 'knew' will be what the questioner 'believes'. The limit of what he would say that he knew, knew empirically was, namely, that psychologically we are god-referring creatures and, given the archetypal quality of the Self, we live with the challenging paradox that the opposite is also true. 'The conscious realization of the self as a paradoxical human whole and a paradoxical God-image was for Jung the cultural and religious task of modern man, constellated by the spirit of the age.'[9] From that it follows that our so human condition has a fundamental need to be expressed in rites of one kind or another, at crossroads and in face of the incomprehensible when we seek reassurance and guidance as to our values and direction.

Rituals mark some of the most solemn occasions of human existence but also some of the most festive and joyous. The labours of the best minds of centuries may have been employed in design of the rites but there are also rites no less beautiful and touching which have sprung forth spontaneously. They continue to do so, especially today and in the aftermath of soul-shattering experiences.

Somewhere in my home there is a faded photograph of a lake at the foot of a snow-draped mountain in the Sierra Nevada range of California, a place that is reached by several days of walking and climbing. And to the photograph are attached lines penned by Nancy Newhall:

> Were all learning lost, all music stilled,
> Man, if these resources still remain to him,
> Could again hear singing in himself
> And rebuild anew the habitations of his thought.[10]

These lines have often been quoted by ecologists and used in support and preservation of our wilderness. I have felt moved to respond to such appeals but as many years ago as when I first saw that lake and read her words, I perceived (though at the time I could not have articulated what I perceived) that what Nancy Newhall was talking about was a god-image; that the wilderness symbolized her church and that the presence of mountain, rock and water suggested the generative encounter with the sacred made possible by ritual pilgrimage, ascent, stillness and reverence. She believed in the power of the Infinite to regenerate meaning but she also feared man's ability to destroy the infinite in himself by disregard of its necessity.

Whether or not she did so consciously, she pointed directly to our human propensity for destruction of the seedbed of our symbols. Rightly, I feel, she foresaw that when this happens, the result is a living death of which we are the perpetrators. She intuited ritual death as the shadow of a humanity lived in denial of other than material values and to the exclusion of symbols wherewith we have the possibility of discovering and recycling those values.

What would happen if ritual died? The result has often been described for us, poetically and symbolically. Singers forget their songs. Storytellers no longer remember their tales. We act out the myths that are telling our lives. Models replace mysteries. Answers take the place of questions. Eventually we lose the thread of significance and are left wandering in a labyrinth of meaninglessness. There may be individuality but there can be no individuation for there is no longer a meeting point between the real and the not-yet-realized in ourselves. There would no longer be men or women of God either, nor could I recognize the Divine in my neighbour. Life would revert to an impersonal and archetypal struggle.

This situation is one with which many can empathize and some will say its time is now. But, of course, ritual does not die. Where there are humans there will be gods and where there are gods there will be ritual. The urge for it is deeply embedded in the psychic matrix of humanity and, being a part of psyche, it behaves as if it were to go on living. Ritual does not die though it can be neglected, trivialized, misused and to some extent ignored. Yet, if desacralized and cut off from psychic awareness, its motive force, the image of the Holy, reverts to unconsciousness, while existing observances become repetitious and sterile.

What is less often emphasized is that so, too, does the image of person drop from consciousness as well. Ritual death, which involves conscious or unconscious denial of its place and function, obliterates not only the vision of God but also that of the unique man or woman. It would be for that reason that, if ritual died, I would no longer recognize the sacred in my neighbour or have compassion for my neighbour as myself. I would not defend my neighbour's rights and privileges as I would my own or be moved to tears by anyone's suffering.

There are events and times, of course, that temporarily and at cost of great pain, blind us to such visions of the Holy as part of our lives but, also, to some extent, again, the choice is ours. We may be able to retain an attitude conducive to consciousness even when consciousness itself is denied. This, of course, is to exist with faith. That, I believe, is our freedom and our task. What we seek by way of ritual engagement is an equivalent to the urgency of a relationship to a situation that will be more than we can express by commitment alone; it is radical and passionate involvement.

An attitude of passionate involvement with the sacred is itself life-enhancing to our person and a religious one. It approaches the eye of the cross without certainty of transformation or assurance that the encounter will be the same as we envisage, yielding what we most sincerely long for at the moment. If we are honest with ourselves we know that the outcome cannot be effected by our personal egos alone or programmed ahead of time. This would amount to the hybris of assuming that we ourselves were all that mattered in its making. 'Invited or not, the god will be present.' And the god as well as our enemy, the Athenians (our neuroses, our partners, our rebellious children, our enterprises, our regrets, our illnesses, our bereavements), must be faced. But the transforming power of a symbolic exchange is assured. We can have faith in that knowledge and wait, and ponder.

Today, our enemies; the marital problems, the pain of illness, the poverty and loneliness of separation along with the fear of random violence associated with an uncertain future, are most often brought to a psychotherapist rather than to an altar and placed before God. Yet, whenever we work therapeutically, we inescapably work religiously – we cannot help it; we are dealing with very old gods newly manifest in ourselves and others. So, it becomes a vital matter what kind of psychology the therapist practises and what our own attitudes are in face of these changing images and towards the ritual healing they require.

For ritual can be seen as a form of piety that is exquisitely adapted to enable us to articulate and make manageable these urgent exchanges having to do with the nature of power and the interaction between power and human problems which are at the heart of change. Only forms which acknowledge the grandeur and the misery of those processes can do justice to so potentially hazardous an enterprise as human growth. Prescriptions are not enough, nor are reasons or mesmerizing incantations. But ritual can render accessible and malleable seemingly inexorable procedures, and bridges with the breath of meaning the great distances between the opposites of what someone *has* been and what he or she *can* become 'if it's in the situation and in yourself'. I often have to ask myself whether, as a therapist, I have the humility and fortitude to stand with a person through the rite of discovering what's in a situation and in himself or herself.

I can be assured, however, that rather than rationally, those answers will appear in the form of metaphor first of all. And, since it's never possible to exclude symbol from life because the unnoticed symbol can always be found in projection somewhere, I also ask whether it is lack of consciousness, as is often stated, that is at the root of ritual and personal suffering or whether it is not also an absence of respect for the irrational and its expression which stands in the way of renewal. I would equate that respect with awe and a willingness for reflection such as that to which Jung enjoins us and Saint Maximos also with his words: 'Without natural contemplation no-one can appreciate the disparity between the symbols through which the Law is expressed and the divine realities which these symbols represent.'[11] And he goes on to make his point with the most telling of examples:

> So long as [a person] cleaves to the letter [of the law], his own inner hunger for spiritual knowledge will not be satisfied; for *he has condemned himself* like the wily serpent to feed on the earth – that is, on the outward and literal form . . . and does not . . . feed on heaven.

Natural contemplation or reflection mediate and differentiate between figurative representations of the truth and Truth itself. It was upon observation of this theory that analytical psychology was founded and this alone distinguishes it from all other psychologies. We who practise it are prepared to recognize that within the undefined space that occurs in the interim between receipt of the symbol and its integration, while it is internally interpreted, something shifts in the personality, an ontological change of being that is registered. And in that psychological process, there is a replay of ritual encounter. What we see later is only an outer manifestation which differs with each individual.

Brought to the crossroads, where creative freedom is a choice, at the juxtaposition of human and divine energies, space is required for contemplation of the mystery of revelation. This space will be imbued with symbolic presence and respect for that presence determines the outcome. For the symbol does not disguise; it reveals over time.[12] Attentiveness is needed during the process of its unfolding, a certain patience and the willingness to relate to it as something more than oneself though belonging to oneself. Meaning follows.

Ritual is the name we give to what happens in that hazardous space, gives witness and pays homage to an encounter between human and divine forces, an exchange that involves a sharing of attributes, though not of essences. Precisely because of this what happens can only be expressed in imaginative and metaphorical form. Many know the definition of the symbol as 'an intuitive idea that can not yet be formulated in any other or better way'.[13] Further, 'A symbol always pre-supposes that the chosen expression is the best possible description or definition of a relatively unknown fact, *which is none the less known to exist or is postulated as existing.*' [my italics][14] But at another point Jung writes in reference to symbols, 'Their pregnant language cries out to us that they mean more than they say.'[15]

These statements were made from a psychological perspective but symbol can also be defined as a bit of the holy caught by the person, awarded by grace to the individual. By way of it much that we associate with our image of God can be laid hold upon for there it is played out with liberating precision. Whenever and wherever we are made aware of this happening there is a recurrence of rite. There is engagement between conflicting oppositions, intercourse and integration, which is the same as transformation. Through attentive reflection image becomes likeness and rewards us with the confidence of knowing – not for everyone but for ourselves, not forever but sufficiently for now, something more of the nature of our being and that of God, a confidence that is both strengthening and tempering. I believe only what I know and what I know is myself I can believe in. Later, given my active participation in life, what I now believe has the chance to reshape itself into something more adequate, pertinent and comprehensive.

It is clear that the work of the psychologist is unavoidably linked with ritual, though psychotherapists are neither celebrants nor propounders of doctrine. We are merely attendants to psyche or soul. The people who come to us are not usually aware of the lack of ritual process in their lives; they are only aware of the problems that betray its lack.

mutual relationship between onese

being satisfies a natural quest of th

place, significance and individuality.

Ritual serves that need. It too i

human for the abiding identity of the

space is a common soil, at least a co

as the homeland of my unique perso

will be heard as a dialect of an anc

language of the searcher for a relat

Source but by way of it I read the l

The narthex of psyche is the loc

ontological exchange. With or withc

gogue, the encounter that occurs the

only safe container for an encounter

is ritual. The symbol is the visible ex

that links what someone is and what he or she discovers of himself or herself as appropriate and lasting.

Speaking metaphorically, ritual is a window open on one side to the eternal. Before it the psychologist stands alongside another, committed to companionship with psyche or soul. The task is seeing through. What will be perceived is not an object of intellectual knowledge, nor the God of the theologian; it will be a god-image ever-revealing, a vision which surpasses both intellect and the senses, a vision which beckons towards the unceasing and infinite transformation of created being.

Ritual is forged to safeguard crossings and in ritual life rehearses for death. Faith in the preservation of ritual expresses trust in process and reinforces an intuition that in endings there are also beginnings. It expresses a deep-seated human longing for continuity and significance to outlive that which must die, give way in preparation for what is waiting to become. Within its circumscribed and sanctified space I meet and am met, challenged and blessed by contact with a wondrous, enigmatic and divine *other*, experienced as present both without and within. In the encounter there is a sharing of mutual values.

The rite like theatre will ever remain a half-open statement, a half-open question. It is ours to complete its message. So far as psyche is concerned, the play is never finished. It is neither statement nor narrative but a vast, complex, coherent poem designed for contemplation of a truth which contains both question and an answer that will always be related to the burning issues of our time. The meaning is for the moment of our performance in which we become aware both of what is expressed and the skill of the creators; form and content merge, coloured by an honesty that bears witness to what we apprehend as our role.

Notes

CHAPTER 1 MADE BY MEDIA

1 Richard Kearney (ed.) *The Irish Mind: Exploring Intellectual Traditions* (Wolfhound Press, Dublin, 1985), p.33.
2 Erik H. Erikson, *Young Man Luther: A Study in Psychoanalysis and History* (Faber and Faber, London, 1958), p.14.
3 Gaston Bachelard, *The Poetics of Reverie: Childhood Language and the Cosmos*, trans. Daniel Russell (Beacon Press, Boston, 1971), p.7.
4 Walter F. Otto, *The Homeric Gods*, trans. Moses Hadas (Thames and Hudson, London, n.d.), p.122.
5 Jacques Barzun, 'The paradoxes of creativity', in Harry A. Wilmer (ed.) *Creativity: Paradoxes and Reflections* (Chiron Publications, Wilmette, 1991), p.13.
6 Ibid., p.6.
7 Sidney Bernstein, 'Granada', quoted by Jeremy Isaacs, interviewed by Peter Froedman, Media page, *The Independent*, 7 June 1989.
8 Bani Shorter, *An Image Darkly Forming* (Routledge, London, 1987), p.53.
9 C.G. Jung, *Alchemical Studies*, trans. R.F.C. Hull (Collected Works, vol. XIII, Routledge and Kegan Paul, London, 1967), para. 54.
10 Mircea Eliade, *Rites and Symbols of Initiation: The Mysteries of Birth and Rebirth* (Harper and Row, New York, 1958), p.7.
11 Joseph Campbell, *The Flight of the Wild Gander: Explorations in the Mythological Dimension* (The Viking Press, New York, 1969), p.156.
12 William Willeford, *Feeling, Imagination, and the Self: Transformations of the Mother–Infant Relationship* (Northwestern University Press, Evanston, 1987), p.39.
13 J.W. Goethe, *The Fisher*, quoted in G. Van der Leeuw, *Religion in Essence and Manifestation: A Study in Phenomenology*, trans. Richard Turner (George Allen and Unwin Ltd., London, 1938), p.463.

CHAPTER 2 INSTANT LITURGY?

1 'Being fully present and making choices between ways of life', part of an unpublished manuscript, *Transformation: Its Theory and Prac-*

tice in Personal, Political, Historical and Sacred Being by Manfred Halpern, forthcoming. Alongside my practice as an Analytical Psychologist, having the privilege of reading this manuscript and discussing it with the author has been a core experience in the evolution of this book.

2 Dorothea Tanning, *Birthday* (The Lapis Press, Santa Monica, San Francisco, 1986), p.165.
3 George Steiner, *After Babel: Aspects of Language and Translation* (Oxford University Press, New York, 1975), p.45.
4 C.G. Jung, *The Spirit in Man, Art and Literature*, trans. R.F.C. Hull (Collected Works, vol. XV, Routledge and Kegan Paul, London, 1971), para. 105.
5 Van der Leeuw, op. cit., p.447.
6 Ian T. Ramsey, *Models and Mystery* (Oxford University Press, London, 1964), p.53ff.
7 See entry on 'Magic', Andrew Samuels, Bani Shorter and Fred Plaut, *A Critical Dictionary of Jungian Analysis* (Routledge and Kegan Paul, London and New York, 1986).
8 Barzun in Wilmer, op. cit., p.13.
9 James Hillman, *Re-visioning Psychology* (Harper and Row Publishers, New York, Evanston, San Francisco, London, 1975), p.13.
10 Ibid., p.14.
11 Ibid., p.15.

CHAPTER 3 THEATRE OF THE SOUL

1 Jerzy Grotowski, *Towards a Poor Theatre*, edited by Eugenio Barba with a preface by Peter Brook (Eyre Methuen Ltd., London, 1978), p.17.
2 Ibid., p.18.
3 Aniela Jaffé, *The Myth of Meaning: Jung and the Expansion of Consciousness*, trans. R.F.C. Hull (Penguin Books Inc., New York, 1975), p.146.
4 Grotowski, op. cit., p.21.
5 James Roose-Evans, *Experimental Theatre from Stanislavsky to Peter Brook* (Routledge, London, 1989), p.106.
6 Ann and Barry Ulanov, *The Witch and the Clown* (Chiron Publications, Wilmette, 1990), p.284.
7 W.A. Dyrness, *Rouault: A Vision of Suffering and Salvation* (William B. Eerdmans, Grand Rapids, 1971), pp.149, 157.
8 Halpern, op. cit., Section II, p.23.
9 Samuels, Shorter and Plaut, op. cit., p.32.
10 Ulanov and Ulanov, op. cit., p.188.
11 Grotowski, op. cit., p.22.
12 Jane Harrison, *Prolegomena to the Study of Greek Religion* (Merlin Press, London, 1980), p.223.
13 Victor Turner, *Dramas, Fields and Metaphors: Symbolic Action in Human Society* (Cornell University Press, Ithaca and London, 1974), p.29.

14 Heinrich Zimmer, *The King and the Corpse: Tales of the Soul's Conquest of Evil*, edited by Joseph Campbell (Princeton University Press, Princeton, 1973), pp.67–87.
15 C.G. Jung, *Civilization in Transition*, trans. R.F.C. Hull (Collected Works, vol. X, Routledge and Kegan Paul, London, 1970), para. 363.
16 Luigi Pirandello, *Six Characters in Search of an Author*, trans. John Linstrum (Methuen Drama, London, 1990), p.10.
17 Joseph Campbell, *The Inner Reaches of Outer Space: Metaphor as Myth and as Religion* (Harper and Row, New York, 1986), p.132.
18 Paul Claudel, quoted in Jean-Louis Barrault, *Memories for Tomorrow: The Memoirs of Jean-Louis Barrault*, trans. Jonathan Griffin (Thames and Hudson, London, 1974), p.184.

CHAPTER 4 THE RITE OF CREATIVITY

1 Nicholas Berdyaev, *Truth and Revelation*, trans. R.M. French (Harper and Brothers, New York, n.d.), p.19.
2 Vladimir Lossky, *The Mystical Theology of the Eastern Church* (James Clarke and Co. Ltd., Cambridge and London, 1973), p.98.
3 Ben Willis, *The Tao of Art: The Inner Meaning of Chinese Art and Philosophy* (Century, London, 1987), p.7.
4 Li K'an, 'Essay on bamboo painting', quoted, ibid., p.4.
5 Bani Shorter, 'Border People' (Guild Lecture no. 211, Guild of Pastoral Psychology, London), p.16.
6 Willis, op. cit., p.84.
7 Rollo May, *The Courage to Create* (Collins, London, 1976), p.105.
8 Kent Johnson and Stephen M. Ashby (eds) *Third Wave: The New Russian Poetry* (The University of Michigan Press, Ann Arbor, 1992), p.129.
9 Sarah Kent and Jacqueline Morreau (eds) *Women's Images of Men* (Writers and Readers Publishing, London, 1985), p.121.
10 Direct reference unknown. Attributed to Joseph Campbell and used as descriptive of consciousness which he defined not only as knowledge, but knowledge fuelled by life energy. See Joseph Campbell with Bill Moyers, *The Power of Myth* (Doubleday, New York, 1988), p.14ff.
11 See Van der Leeuw, op. cit., pp.306 and 499.
12 Willis, op. cit., p.84.
13 May, op. cit., p.40.
14 René Malamud, 'The Amazon problem', in James Hillman *et al.*, *Facing the Gods* (Spring Publications, Inc., Irving, 1980), p.47.
15 Willis, op. cit., p.82.
16 Victor Turner, *The Ritual Process: Structure and Anti-Structure* (Cornell University Press, Ithaca, 1969), p.7.
17 Willis, op. cit., p.121.

CHAPTER 5 LISTENING TO SUBJECTIVITY

1 Berdyaev, op. cit., p.75.
2 Martin Heidegger, *Poetry, Language, Thought*, translations and introduction by Albert Hofstadter (Harper and Row Publishers, New
York, London, 1975), 'Letter of 18 June 1950', p.123.
3 Campbell, *Flight of the Wild Gander*, op. cit., p.180.
4 Jung, *Civilization in Transition*, (CW X), op. cit., para. 509.
5 Rainer Maria Rilke, *Duino Elegies*, translation, introduction and commentary by J.B. Leishman and Stephen Spender (W.W. Norton and
Company, Inc., New York, 1939), 'The Ninth Elegy', lines 44–6, p.75.
6 Heidegger, op. cit., p.127.
7 Attention has been called to this lack notably in the numerous writings of James Hillman (Analytical Psychologist/Archetypal
Psychologist), Manfred Halpern (Political Scientist, Professor Emeri-
tus, Princeton University) and Andrew Samuels (Analytical Psychologist. See especially *The Political Psyche*, Routledge, London,
1993).
8 Here notable exceptions have been Adolf Guggenbühl-Craig
(Psychiatrist/Analytical Psychologist. See especially *Power in the
Helping Professions*, Spring Publications, New York, 1971), Rafael
López-Pedraza (Analytical Psychologist. See *Cultural Anxiety*,
Daimon Verlag, Einsiedelu, 1990) and Anthony Stevens (Psychiatrist/
Analytical Psychologist. See *The Roots of War: A Jungian Perspective*,
Paragon House Publishers, New York, 1989).
9 See James Hillman, 'Schism as differing visions', in *Loose Ends*
(Spring Publications, Zurich, 1975).
10 Don Cupitt, *What Is a Story?* (SCM Press Ltd., London, 1991), p.63.
11 Hillman, op. cit., p.89.
12 Paul Tillich quoted in May, op. cit., p.35. See also Willeford, op.
cit., p.414: '... nonbeing as the ground of being is embodied in the
philosophy of Schelling, or the "God beyond God" of the theologian
Paul Tillich ... or the Void of the Buddhists'. Willeford, an Analytical
Psychologist, cites this as analagous to a young child's experience of
developing consciousness: '... as consciousness develops, feeling and
imagination remain open to the self and able to find intimations of
its life in even the nothing of silence and the hints of undefined
somethings within it'.
13 Karl Jaspers, referred to by Rollo May, *The Discovery of Being,
Writings in Existential Psychology* (W.W. Norton and Company, New
York and London, 1983), p.15.
14 Victor Turner and Edith Turner, *Image and Pilgrimage in Christian
Culture: Anthropological Perspectives* (Columbia University Press,
New York, 1978), p.15.
15 Ibid., p.11.
16 Colin Morris, BBC Sunday Programme, 12 March 1995.
17 Dyrness, op. cit., p.74.
18 James Hillman, 'Senex and puer', in James Hillman *et al.*, *Puer Papers*
(Spring Publications, Inc., Irving, 1979), p.7.

19 Hillman, ibid., p.6.
20 Cupitt, op. cit., p.70.
21 Grotowski, op. cit., p.17.

CHAPTER 6 PRISONER OF A THOUSAND FACES

1 Van der Leeuw, op. cit., p.225.
2 D.H. Lawrence, *The Complete Poems of D.H. Lawrence*, collected and edited with an introduction and notes by Vivian de Sola Pinto and Warren Roberts, vol. II (Heinemann, London, 1972), p. 620.
3 Lossky, op. cit., p.30.
4 C.G. Jung, *Psychology and Religion: West and East*, trans. R.F.C. Hull (Collected Works, vol. XI, Routledge and Kegan Paul, London, 1969), para. 400.
5 Ibid.
6 Lossky, op. cit., p.132.
7 C.G. Jung, *Psychology and Alchemy*, trans. R.F.C. Hull (Collected Works, vol. XII, Routledge and Kegan Paul, London, 1968), para. 152.
8 Jung, *Psychology and Religion* (Collected Works, vol. XI), ibid., para 745.
9 Van der Leeuw, op. cit., p.490.
10 Willeford, op. cit., p.88.
11 Fritjof Capra, *The Turning Point: Science, Society, and the Rising Culture* (Harper Collins Publishers, London, 1983), p.87.
12 Peter Brown, *The Cult of the Saints* (University of Chicago Press, Chicago, 1981), p.50.
13 Ibid., p.51.
14 Willeford, op. cit., p. 88.
15 Mark C. Taylor, *Journeys to Selfhood: Hegel and Kierkegaard* (University of California Press, Berkeley and Los Angeles, 1980), p.253.
16 Nancy Stark Smith, 'Taking no for an answer', *Contact Quarterly*, vol. XII, no. 2, quoted in Miranda Tufnell and Chris Crickmay, *Body, Space, Image* (Dance Books Ltd., London, 1993), p.193.

CHAPTER 7 IF RITUAL DIES

1 Shorter, 'Border People', op. cit., p.19.
2 Monica Wilson, 'Nyakyusa ritual and symbolism', *American Anthropologist*, vol. 56, no. 2, quoted in Turner, *The Ritual Process*, op. cit., p.6. See also Samuels, Shorter and Plaut, op. cit., entry on 'Ritual'.
3 Peter Brown, *Society and the Holy in Late Antiquity* (Faber and Faber, London, 1982), p.6.
4 Shorter, *An Image Darkly Forming*, op. cit., p.44ff.
5 James Hillman, *Suicide and the Soul* (Harper and Row, New York, 1973), p.178.
6 C.G. Jung, *Two Essays on Analytical Psychology*, trans. R.F.C. Hull

(Collected Works, vol. VII, Routledge and Kegan Paul, London, 1966), para. 71ff.

7 Ibid., para. 399.

8 Peter Brook, *The Empty Space* (Penguin Books Ltd., Harmondsworth, 1982), p.62.

9 Jaffé, op. cit., p.120.

10 Ansel Adams, *Ansel Adams: An Autobiography* (Little Brown and Company, Boston, 1985), p.217.

11 Translated from the Greek and edited by G.E.H. Palmer, Philip Sherrard and Kallistos Ware, *The Philokalia*, vol. II (Faber and Faber, London and Boston, 1981), p.268.

12 C.G. Jung, *The Symbolic Life*, trans. R.F.C. Hull (Collected Works, vol. XVIII, Routledge and Kegan Paul, London, 1977), para. 483.

13 Jung, *The Spirit in Man, Art and Literature* (Collected Works, vol. XV), op. cit., para. 105.

14 C.G. Jung, *Psychological Types*, trans. R.F.C. Hull (Collected Works, vol. VI, Routledge and Kegan Paul, London, 1971), para. 814.

15 Jung, *The Spirit in Man, Art and Literature* (Collected Works, vol. XV), op. cit., para. 119.

Index

absolution 65
acausal phenomena 109
acceptance 22, 43, 66, 87, 99, 103, 104
acedia 95
acting-out 37, 61, 63, 116
actor 40–52, 55, 60, 63, 84, 93
adaptation 57, 79, 99, 106
Aeschylus 48
aggression 29
alienation 9, 37, 84, 91–2, 106
Allah 113
allegory 54, 85
aloneness 21, 67, 102
Amazons 70; *see also* Shields of the Amazons
amplification 10, 61, 70, 75
analysis 1, 3–4, 7, 8, 15, 16, 26, 39, 64, 67, 74, 75, 78, 97–100
analyst 2, 4–9, 17, 25, 58, 63, 64, 73, 75, 96
Analytical Psychology 25, 26; distinguishing concept of 119
anima 11, 13, 14, 16, 17
animism 37
animus 9, 16
anthropological technique 75
anxiety 50, 81, 91, 102
apathy 33, 66
archetype 9, 12–16, 20, 23, 24, 26, 28, 29, 32, 37–46, 50, 52, 59, 60, 63, 76, 78, 85, 88, 94, 104, 108, 112, 117; of the ego 92; of Great Mother and Old Patriarch 16; of

life (anima) 14; of the self 41, 73, 74, 115; of the shadow 64; of transformation 85, 95
art 21, 36, 58, 62–9, 84; the arts 65
artist 58–71, 88; role of 59
ascetic practice 70
Athenians 111, 118
authority 20, 22, 24, 32, 60, 61, 77, 89, 90, 91, 97
autonomous psychic contents 12
avoidance 29, 50, 98, 108
awakening 25, 64; 'Wake up!' 115
awareness 2, 4, 5, 11, 12, 15, 23, 41, 47, 48, 50, 52, 59–63, 65, 77–9, 83–5, 88, 111–14, 117
awe 28, 41, 45, 62, 99, 118

Bachelard, Gaston 4
balance 73, 74, 76, 80, 85, 90, 95, 111
baptism 55, 94, 109
Barzun, Jacques 6
Beethoven, Ludwig van 97
befriending 88, 101, 104; the dream 55
being 8, 10, 12, 16, 22–6, 31, 32, 34, 37, 38, 41, 43, 44, 46, 48, 59–64, 68, 71, 74, 79, 82, 93, 95, 97, 110–12, 119–21
belief 38, 45, 48, 50, 77, 78, 80, 81, 94, 102, 112, 115, 120
blasphemy 31
border 24, 27, 44, 47, 69, 93, 95, 96, 99, 111